Procter & Gamble Educational Services

Advisory Committee

Procter & Gamble Educational Services acknowledges, with special thanks, the many thoughtful and constructive suggestions given us by the following Home Economics professionals. Their assistance has been given as individuals, not as representatives of any organization.

Jane G. Arnold
Supervisor Home Economics
Cincinnati Public Schools
Cincinnati, Ohio

Joan A. Becker
Home Economics Teacher
 & Department Chair
Withrow High School
Cincinnati, Ohio

Ruth E. Dohner
Assistant Professor
Dept. of Home Economics Education
College of Home Economics
The Ohio State University
Columbus, Ohio

Lynda J. Heyl
Home Economics Consultant
Columbus, Ohio

Alicia Kelley
Homemaking Teacher
Western Hills High School
Cincinnati, Ohio

Naurine R. McCormick
Home Economics Extension,
Associate Dean Emeritus
College of Home Economics
The Ohio State University
Columbus, Ohio

Alice T. Miskell
Home Economics Consultant
Columbus, Ohio

Vera M. Ramstetter
Associate Director of Vocational
 Education
Cincinnati Public Schools
Cincinnati, Ohio

Gemelia Tyler
Vocational Home Economics Teacher
 & Department Head
Hillsboro High School
Hillsboro, Ohio

Special contributors to the development of these materials were:

Kathy Lyter
Manager, Home Economics
Laundry & Home Care Products
Procter & Gamble
Cincinnati, Ohio

Ralph Zeuthen
Editorial Consultant
New York, New York

Jean Learn

Jean Learn
Program Manager
Educational Services
Procter & Gamble

THE HOW TO CLEAN HANDBOOK

making easier work of laundering, cleaning and dishwashing

Copyright © 1986 by Procter & Gamble Educational Services

All rights reserved. No part of this work may be reproduced or transmitted in any form or by any means, electronic or mechanical, including photocopying and recording, or by any information storage or retrieval system, except by permission. Requests for permission should be addressed in writing to, Procter & Gamble Educational Services, P.O. Box 599, Cincinnati, Ohio 45201.

Printed in the U.S.A.

Library of Congress Catalog Card Number: 86-61512

ISBN: 0-938973-00-2

Table of Contents

Introduction   Page ix

     Profound changes in the way people live have brought a new way to look at many household activities. This introduction notes that busy lives outside the home have put a premium on time and energy; it suggests that the best way to handle such chores as laundering, cleaning and dishwashing is to manage them better, and tells how.

Chapter 1   **How to Accentuate the Positives, Save Time and Get Better Results**   Page 1

     The first step is to get ourselves into a positive frame of mind about the rather unglamorous chores of laundering, cleaning and dishwashing. This chapter shows how to accentuate the positives, then outlines six ways to organize this work. Getting started on the right foot will get better results, save time, even boost our egos a bit.

Chapter 2   **How to Choose the Right Product**   Page 11

     Whatever the task, using the right product is one of the keys. You don't have to be an expert, but it pays to know a few basic facts about product ingredients and how they work. You will learn why it is a good idea to: read information on product packages, use advertising to your advantage in selecting products and call manufacturers' toll-free telephone lines when you have a question.

Chapter 3   **How to Organize Your Laundering**   Page 33

     Is anything more maddening than a stubborn stain? Experts tell us how to deal with a variety of stains common to most households. You will also find nine simple rules to help organize the laundering effort—from tips on sorting clothes, to reading care labels, to hanging, folding and storing laundered items neatly. Covers both machine and hand laundering. The correct procedure easily becomes second nature.

Chapter 4   **How to Clean Hard Surfaces**   Page 107

     Count the hard surfaces in your home—floors, counter tops, etc. There may be as many as 20 different types, each a cleaning problem unto itself. Here we need expert advice. Experts have assembled two helpful lists—the products that fit these jobs, and how to clean the surfaces. The particular information you need is easily located on quick-reference charts.

Chapter 5 ***How to Plan Better Dishwashing***   Page 137

           Dishwashing is something we do every day. Here's a little test for yourself: How many of the six steps to better dishwashing listed in this chapter do you routinely follow? There are also five expert, quick-reference charts that can help you get organized and do a better, more efficient job, whether by machine or hand.

Chapter 6 ***The Consumer and P&G . . . Creating the Right Product Together***   Page 171

           Many people are surprised to learn how products come to be created. At Procter & Gamble consumers participate every step of the way. Through a variety of research techniques, consumers describe their habits and needs as a guide to P&G's product development people, then help test and re-test products. Consumers and company alike benefit from this never-ending dialogue.

Chapter 7 ***Frequently Asked Questions (and Their Answers)***   Page 177

           Do you ever have questions like these? Why bother to use a fabric softener? How should I clean my fiberglass bathtub? Each year, about a million people ask questions like these of Procter & Gamble. This chapter answers 21 popular questions and invites you to ask your questions.

Chapter 8 ***A Little Romance***   Page 189

           Colorful legends that take us back thousands of years show that laundering took its first step forward with the accidental discovery of "soap." The slow progress from primitive soap to the first detergent, then the rapid advancement of modern products, offer a delightful bit of history.

—Glossary of Terms   Page 193

—Additional References   Page 224

Charts

1.1	*Guide for General Home Care*	Chapter 1	Page 6
1.2	*Guide for Clothing Care and Laundering*	Chapter 1	Page 8
2.1	*Ingredients in Laundering, Cleaning and Dishwashing Products*	Chapter 2	Page 22
2.2	*Product Categories*	Chapter 2	Page 31
3.1	*Apparel Care Labeling Guide*	Chapter 3	Page 47
3.2	*Fiber Facts*	Chapter 3	Page 50
3.3	*Special Laundering Instructions*	Chapter 3	Page 60
3.4	*Products for Pretreating or Removing Stains*	Chapter 3	Page 79
3.5	*Stain Removal Guide for Washable Items*	Chapter 3	Page 80
3.6	*Laundry Products and Aids*	Chapter 3	Page 86
3.7	*Laundering Problems . . . Causes, Solutions, Preventive Measures*	Chapter 3	Page 96
4.1	*Cleaning Hard Surfaces in the Home*	Chapter 4	Page 112
4.2	*Household Cleaning Products*	Chapter 4	Page 128
5.1	*Dishwashing Products and Aids*	Chapter 5	Page 144
5.2	*Hand Dishwashing Supplies*	Chapter 5	Page 149
5.3	*Hand Dishwashing Problems . . . Causes and Solutions*	Chapter 5	Page 150
5.4	*Cleaning Dishwashable Items*	Chapter 5	Page 152
5.5	*Dishwasher Problems . . . Causes, Solutions, Preventive Measures*	Chapter 5	Page 162

INTRODUCTION

This book has been written to show you how to make laundering, cleaning and dishwashing much easier on your back, your time, your temper and your pocketbook. And it may do small wonders for your ego, too.

These pages are packed with practical, thoroughly-tested ideas. They are not magic, but they work. They are presented here, in everyday language, along with easy-to-use, problem-solving charts.

The material that follows has a single-minded purpose: to give women, men and teenagers—the modern cast of characters in housework—a sensible way to save time and energy on the toughest household chores by applying simple management skills, mixing brains and brawn. (Everybody has the basic management skills; this book tells how to use them.)

Why this new book just now? Because time and energy have become such scarce commodities in the modern home. We live far more active lives than before, as each new generation does, and much of our living takes place away from home. Gone are the times, gone and unmourned, when the cleaning and laundering burdens fell automatically on the shoulders of women because they spent their time primarily at home.

Women still clean and launder; there is no escaping the inevitable. But men, through choice or necessity, are carrying more of the load. So are teenagers. Also, single men and women, most working at outside jobs, have set up their own homes, with nobody to do the cleaning and laundering but themselves. Many of these people are new to the process, relatively unsophisticated and in need of experienced guidance.

Not that this handbook has forgotten experienced homemakers. Or professionals. Products and standard practices, second nature for both, have changed a bit, for the better. They will also find new ideas here, along with the solid basics that never change.

As different as they are, all these people—men, women, experienced, inexperienced—have two things indisputably in common: they are busy, and most don't exactly love housework.

Too little time creates a cleaning crisis for all too often.

This book takes the position that the best way to cut down household work to a manageable size is to do what any person in business would do: *organize it*. Define the job to be done. Get the necessary equipment. Decide which job comes first. Set aside a certain time each week for this work. Set a time limit for getting each job done. Read information on packages and follow directions explicitly. Avoid false starts when you don't have materials to get the job done. Finish what you start.

This is the kind of management planning you will find in this book, in text and charts, to which you can add your own management ideas.

Keep the book handy for easy reference and consult it when in doubt. In no time at all, you will form the habit of organizing your cleaning and laundering and dishwashing, squeezing out wasted minutes, making economical use of materials and giving your home a noticeably better look.

Not magic, perhaps, but it will do small wonders for your home . . . and for your ego.

THE
HOW TO
CLEAN
HANDBOOK

1 How to Accentuate the Positives, Save Time and Get Better Results

And where better to start than with this first recommendation: Organize your attitude toward these tasks before you do anything else.

This book tells how to organize your laundering, cleaning and dishwashing, as any good manager would.

And where better to start than with this first recommendation: *Organize your attitude toward these tasks before you do anything else.*

Despite the pleasure we take when all is fresh and clean in our homes, this kind of work has long suffered something of an image problem. While many people enjoy such creative work as cooking and decorating—and talk animatedly about them—cleaning and laundering are usually doggedly done and forgotten and, when talked about at all, put down as chores.

Chores they may be, because we can't wish them away or postpone them for weeks or months to a more convenient time. And doing these chores week after week takes the edge off the novelty that comes with work done only occasionally, when the spirit moves us.

Accentuate The Positives

The best way to view laundering, cleaning and dishwashing is to organize your attitude by accentuating the positives:

- The time you devote to this work can be spent either by yourself (a blessing after a long day at your job) or shared

1

with others in the home. If you have carefully organized the tasks, your mind can be free to think about other things.

- Cleaning done systematically, on a well-organized schedule, has a way of keeping the home neat. The worst thing is to allow messiness to pile up, for sooner or later you must confront the result with a strenuous effort—the kind that gives cleaning a bad name.

- A clean and orderly home can mean fewer health problems and accidents. Cluttered passageways, food particles on kitchen counter and floor, accumulated dust are all so easy to avoid with an organized cleaning program.

- Everybody needs a morale boost now and then, and taking good care of a home and clothing gives you a right to feel good about yourself. It is necessary work and, when done efficiently, the results always look so good. So where's the harm in a little self-appreciation?

- In the most practical sense, caring properly for your clothes and home furnishings is simply a matter of protecting an investment that runs into hundreds of dollars, perhaps even thousands. They will last longer and look better . . . and so will you.

- One of the positive things about setting up an organized program is you can make your own rules for cleaning and laundering. Do these things when they suit your purposes; there is nothing sacred about once-a-week. Decide for yourself how clean you want each room to be, immaculate or lived-in. There is only one rule that should be unbreakable: *organize the work and stick to the plan.*

If there are others in your household—a spouse, a child, a roommate—organizing the laundering, cleaning and dishwashing is almost a necessity. Because two or three lives add enormously to the work to be done, restrict your freedom to choose your time and raise the question of how to split the tasks. If you are lucky enough to have others to help solve the problem they did their share to create, the best way is to work together on a plan spelling out the work each will do, and when—and a solemn agreement to stick to it.

1/How to Accentuate the Positives

Making A Plan

Now, to the plan itself.

The first step is to begin at the logical beginning: Define the jobs to be done. To help you along, Chart 1.1 (Guide for General Home Care), and Chart 1.2 (Guide for Clothing Care and Laundering) on Pages 6-8 list dozens of household tasks that include cleaning, laundering, dishwashing. Consider them a starting point. Then draw on your management skills and lay out this six-point plan:

The first step is to begin at the logical beginning: Define the jobs to be done.

1. *Define the problem.* Use the charts as guides, and list all the jobs that must be done in your home. The situation is different in every home, so begin with the charts and add or subtract jobs as you see fit. The trick is to be thorough; review the list as the weeks go by, in case you have overlooked something. (It is surprising how thorough we are when we have to put things down on paper.)

2. *Set your goal.* How much "clean" do you want? At first, that might sound a bid odd, because everybody wants clothes and home to be spotless. But perfection is the ideal, not the reality, in the busy lives of most people. It is particularly difficult when there are others in the household whose needs and wishes complicate the problem. Here is where your management judgment comes into play. As a practical matter, how much can you expect to accomplish? It is extremely important to have a goal with which to motivate yourself, a standard by which to measure the success of your efforts.

3. *Determine priorities.* Look at your charts. You're a pragmatic manager and know that some problems must get preferential treatment. For example, suppose the clothes you wear to the office are important to your success. If time is tight, and you must choose between caring for your clothes and some other task, your wardrobe will win out.

When making up your charts, it could be helpful to rate each job under headings such as these:
Very important
Important, but not urgent
Nice, but not necessary
The trouble with this idea, practical as it might appear, is there is always the lurking temptation to put more and more items under "Nice, but not necessary." And there goes the plan.

4. *Make out a timetable.* The charts show whether jobs should be done daily, weekly, occasionally or seasonally. Perhaps that is all the timetable you need. But consider going one step further: For the daily and weekly jobs, specify morning, afternoon or evening, and put down the number of minutes you allow for each task. The objective is to establish habits. You'll find these time limits a dependable reminder not to fritter away 45 minutes on a job you usually do in 30. In a busy life, can anything be more important than managing your time?

5. *Make good use of people-power.* In organizing any project, the most basic thing is to make sure everybody knows their job, so no job will go undone in the confusion of vague assignments. When you list the job on your chart, write the name of the person responsible and when the work is to be done. Most people prefer one kind of task to another, and that makes the assigning easy. It is also a good idea to rotate the jobs to ward off boredom. There are a hundred ways to make the best use of your people-power, so adjust as you all gain experience.

6. *Use the right materials.* Once you have organized everything—the problem, goal, priorities, timetable, manpower—there is still one more thing to do. The next chapter tells you how to select the right materials to make easier work of laundering, cleaning and dishwashing.

But, first, you have work to do. Turn to the charts that follow this text. Try to visualize how the lists apply to your home or situation. Then set your own priorities and make your own lists.

In organizing any project, the most basic thing is to make sure everybody knows their job, so no job will go undone in the confusion of vague assignments.

1/How to Accentuate the Positives

Chapter 1

Related Charts

Chart 1.1   Guide for General Home Care
Chart 1.2   Guide for Clothing Care and Laundering

Guide for General Home Care

LIVING AREA	DAILY	WEEKLY
Kitchen	Wash dishes Tidy and wipe counter tops, range and appliances Clean sink Empty garbage Sweep or damp mop floor	Dispose of left-over foods Clean range thoroughly Wipe out refrigerator Thoroughly clean floor Clean garbage pail
Bathroom	Clean wash basin and tub Replace soiled towels Empty wastepaper basket	Wash floor Clean toilet bowl Wipe tile surfaces and accessories Clean toothbrush holder and other fixtures Clean mirrors
Living Room/Family Room	Dispose of papers Straighten magazines, throw pillows and other accessories	Vacuum rugs and upholstered furniture Vacuum or dust floors including baseboards and corners Dust and/or polish furniture Dust and clean lamps, other decorative objects Empty wastepaper baskets
Bedroom	Make beds Put away clothing Straighten dresser tops and accessories	Change bed linens Vacuum Dust and/or polish furniture Dust and clean lamps and other decorative objects Empty wastepaper basket

Chart 1.1

OCCASIONALLY	SEASONALLY
Clean oven, microwave Defrost and clean refrigerator, freezer Wash walls, woodwork and cabinet fronts Clean, wax floor Clean appliances thoroughly Move and clean under and behind furniture	Clean closets, cabinets Wash stored dishes, glasses, linens Wash windows, curtains, blinds or shades Clean screens or storm windows
Wash throw rugs, toilet cover and shower curtain Wash walls, woodwork	Clean closets, cabinets Wash windows, blinds, shades or curtains Clean screens or storm windows
Shampoo rugs and upholstered furniture Wash lamp shades and diffusing bowls, wipe cool bulbs with a damp cloth Move and clean under furniture Clean, wax floors Dust books, pictures Wash walls, woodwork Clean TV screen, mirrors, pictures	Clean closets Wash windows, blinds, shades or curtains Clean screens or storm windows
Organize closets Remove clothing no longer used Turn mattresses Wash mattress pads and covers Air pillows or wash if possible Wash walls, woodwork Move and clean under furniture Clean, wax floors Wash lamp shades and diffusing bowls, wipe cool bulbs with a damp cloth Dust pictures, books	Wash or dryclean blankets, spreads Clean closets Wash windows, blinds, shades or curtains Clean screens or storm windows

Guide for Clothing Care and Laundering — Chart 1.2

DAILY

Empty pockets

Check clothing and separate items that need mending or special treatment

Put soiled clothing in hamper

Air non-washable items

Hang up clothes

WEEKLY

Sort clothes

Mend clothes before washing

Pretreat spots and stains

Wash clothes in washer

Hand wash items as needed

Dry clothes in dryer or air dry

Steam press or iron, as needed

Fold or hang clothes and store them

Take non-washable clothes to drycleaner

Wash bed linens and towels

OCCASIONALLY

Wash sweaters, jackets, scarves, hats, etc, according to manufacturer's directions

Discard or give away clothes that are not worn

SEASONALLY

Wash and store out-of-season clothes

Wash curtains, throw rugs, pillows and other washable home furnishings

Personal Notes

DAILY

WEEKLY

OCCASIONALLY

SEASONALLY

2 How to Choose the Right Product

In order to settle on the right product for each specific task on your schedule, you need to know exactly what kind of cleaning problem you are dealing with on each job.

The first thing to know about choosing the right product is this: The right product will do a better job, save time, cost less and spare you the frustrations and disappointments that can turn a good day upside down. This chapter tells how to make the right choice.

It is time to put your organizational skills to work again.

In Chapter I you made a schedule for all the cleaning, laundering and dishwashing jobs in your home. In order to settle on the right product for each specific task on your schedule, you need to know exactly what kind of cleaning problem you are dealing with on each job. Use the lists you have already made, and add *the nature of the cleaning problem*. Here is an example:

The cleaning job	The nature of the cleaning problem	Type of product needed
Wash kitchen floor	ground-in dirt	(to be filled in later)
Launder beach towels	stained with suntan lotion	
Handwash casserole	baked on food	

After listing specific jobs, write down your description of the nature of the cleaning problem. It is just possible you will find this a helpful exercise, and when you finish you will know more about your household and lifestyle than you could have dreamed. If you have a spouse, roommate or teenager who help with the work and shopping, invite them to join you in making up the list.

(Don't worry about "product needed" just yet. You'll fill that in later and when you do, hang this information on the inside door of the closet where you store your cleaning supplies so you can easily consult it.)

One good reason for this exercise is it forces you to examine your various cleaning jobs until you thoroughly understand them. You will see that one kind of dirt is not the same as all others, and you will understand why the people who manufacture these products offer you such a wide variety.

Actually, when you make this list of jobs and define their nature, you are doing, in a small way, what manufacturers do in a big way. Their researchers talk to thousands upon thousands of householders and document all kinds of cleaning jobs. Their scientists then define the nature of these jobs and create the right products to handle them.

But, you don't have to be a chemist to understand how all these laundering, cleaning and dishwashing products are able to get things clean.

You just need to know there are four basic processes involved in dissolving and removing soil.

1. *Wetting*
Wetting is the first step in cleaning. By itself, water tends to form droplets and rest on top of the surface without penetrating soil. Laundry and cleaning products contain a surface active agent (surfactant) which makes the water spread out evenly and allows the cleaning solution to get between the soil and the surface, loosening and removing the soil.

2. *Emulsifying*
Fats, oils and greasy soils are difficult to dissolve. Emulsifiers are chemicals that break these soils into tiny particles so they can be easily removed from the surface and kept suspended in the wash solution until rinsed away.

You just need to know there are four basic processes involved in dissolving and removing soil.

2/How to Choose the Right Product

3. *Dispersing*

Dispersing is similar to emulsifying but is the term used for solid soil such as mud. By dispersing dirt, the cleaning product keeps the soil finely divided and suspended until rinsed away.

4. *Sequestering*

Sequestering is a chemical reaction that overcomes the effect of the minerals in water. Certain ingredients have the ability to capture or surround these minerals that otherwise would prevent other cleaning product ingredients from dissolving and removing soil.

It is important to have these simple definitions in mind because you will often find them on the package labels when you go shopping. Some of the other product ingredients you may see are listed on Chart 2.1 (Ingredients in Laundering, Cleaning and Dishwashing Products), Pages 22-29.

Choosing a Product Type

Choose the type of product(s) needed for the job(s) you plan to tackle.

What have we accomplished so far?

You have listed your cleaning jobs, described the nature of the cleaning problem for each and learned how soil is removed. That brings us to the third column on your list: *Product needed*. Now begins the actual process of choosing the right product.

For starters, run your eye down the list on Chart 2.2 (Product Categories), Page 31.

The list shows five product categories and 34 types of products. (On your grocer's shelves, many of those 34 types are offered under several brand names. No wonder you have to define the exact nature of your cleaning problem to choose the right one among so many.)

With Chart 2.2 in front of you, choose the type of product(s) needed for the job(s) you plan to tackle. For example, play clothes stained with grass require a detergent with enzymes. That is the type of product you will look for when you are shopping.

Getting Information on Brands

There is a great deal to be learned by reading the package instructions, trying the product and comparing the results with the product you have been using.

Once you have the right *type* of product, you must choose the *brand* that appears likely to do the best job for you. Where do you turn for help?

One source of information is advertising. A television commercial aims to familiarize you with the brand and package. It also often shows the product in action, solving one of your problems—for example, a liquid detergent pretreating stains or heavy soil. A 30-second commercial hardly has time to tell the whole story, but it is surprising how much you can learn in a few blinks of your eye.

Radio also tends to concentrate on a single major point.

Ads in newspapers and magazines, limited by space but not time, go into considerably more detail.

One of the very best ways to see what a product can do is to try it. When a manufacturer mails you a small free sample, read the instructions and use the product. Sometimes samples are handed out in stores or on the street—don't pass them by. Another way manufacturers get you to try the product is to run a coupon in a print ad, offering a regular size package at a reduced price. There is a great deal to be learned by reading the package instructions, trying the product and comparing the results with the product you have been using.

Another source—often quite helpful—is this: When a friend, or relative, or anyone whose opinion you respect, begins to describe his or her experience with a certain product, listen and learn what you can. If your problems are basically the same, such chats can be invaluable.

One more source of information is the manufacturer. Many have Consumer Information Services, some with toll-free telephone numbers. If you need certain information to help make up your mind, call or write, and ask their expert advice. (There is more about Procter & Gamble's Consumer Services operation on Pages 19-20.)

Read the package before buying any product.

Last, but certainly one of the richest mines of information, is the package. Responsible manufacturers are meticulous about the facts on their packages because they want you to use the product correctly to solve a specific problem. They dread the thought of your misusing the product. In addition to usage directions, packages also tell you what the product can be expected to do, list ingredients, state the name and mailing address of the manufacturer. Some packages also include a toll-free "800" telephone number to encourage you to call if you have any questions or comments. (See Pages 16-17, for an illustration of a typical Procter & Gamble detergent package. Also shown is additional package information unique to specific P&G products.) So, read the package before buying any product.

One last thought. What about prices? One brand may cost twice as much per ounce as another. Is the other brand a bargain? Maybe not. Maybe the first brand has more cleaning power, or is more concentrated, so you need less of it. It may seem logical to compare products on a cost-per-ounce basis, but this judgment is not valid. The real cost of a product is its price-per-use.

When all is said and done, the best practice is to choose the product that does the best job for you. You will save money, time and disappointment. That is the payoff for being organized instead of haphazard.

So now the moment has arrived. Make your product choice.

Tips on Storing Products

Now that you have the product in your home, where are you going to store it?

Here is how to approach that question: "I chose the right product, paid a fair price for it. I am going to use it again and

Package

Diagram of a typical Procter

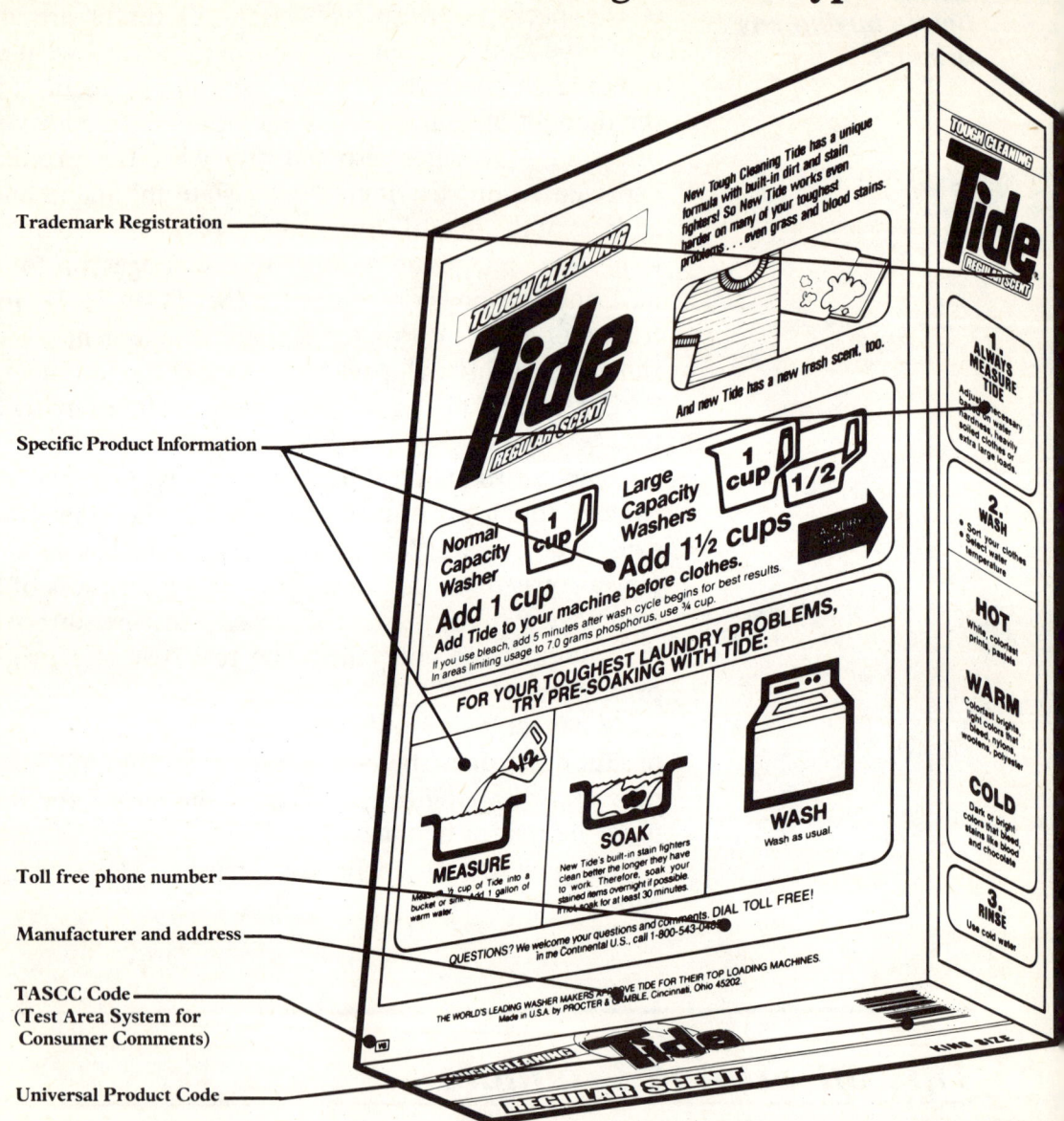

- Trademark Registration
- Specific Product Information
- Toll free phone number
- Manufacturer and address
- TASCC Code (Test Area System for Consumer Comments)
- Universal Product Code

ADDITIONAL LABEL INFORMATION UNIQUE

Indication of change in product formula
Shown when applicable
Examples: "New", "Improved". These terms can be used for only a limited time.

Patent Number
Indicates the manufacturer has exclusive rights to product formula and/or process for making product.
Example: Comet Cleanser - U.S. Patents 3,583,922; 3,715,314; 3,829,385

Active and Inert Ingredients
When a product has disinfecting ability, such as Comet Cleanser, the U.S. Environmental Protection Agency requires the percent of ingredients having this disinfecting property be listed as active. All other ingredients are considered "inert." In this case, "inert" means only those ingredients that do not disinfect. It does not mean the ingredients do not clean. "Inert" ingredients can contribute to the cleaning performance of a product, and very definitely do in the example used here.

Information

& Gamble detergent package

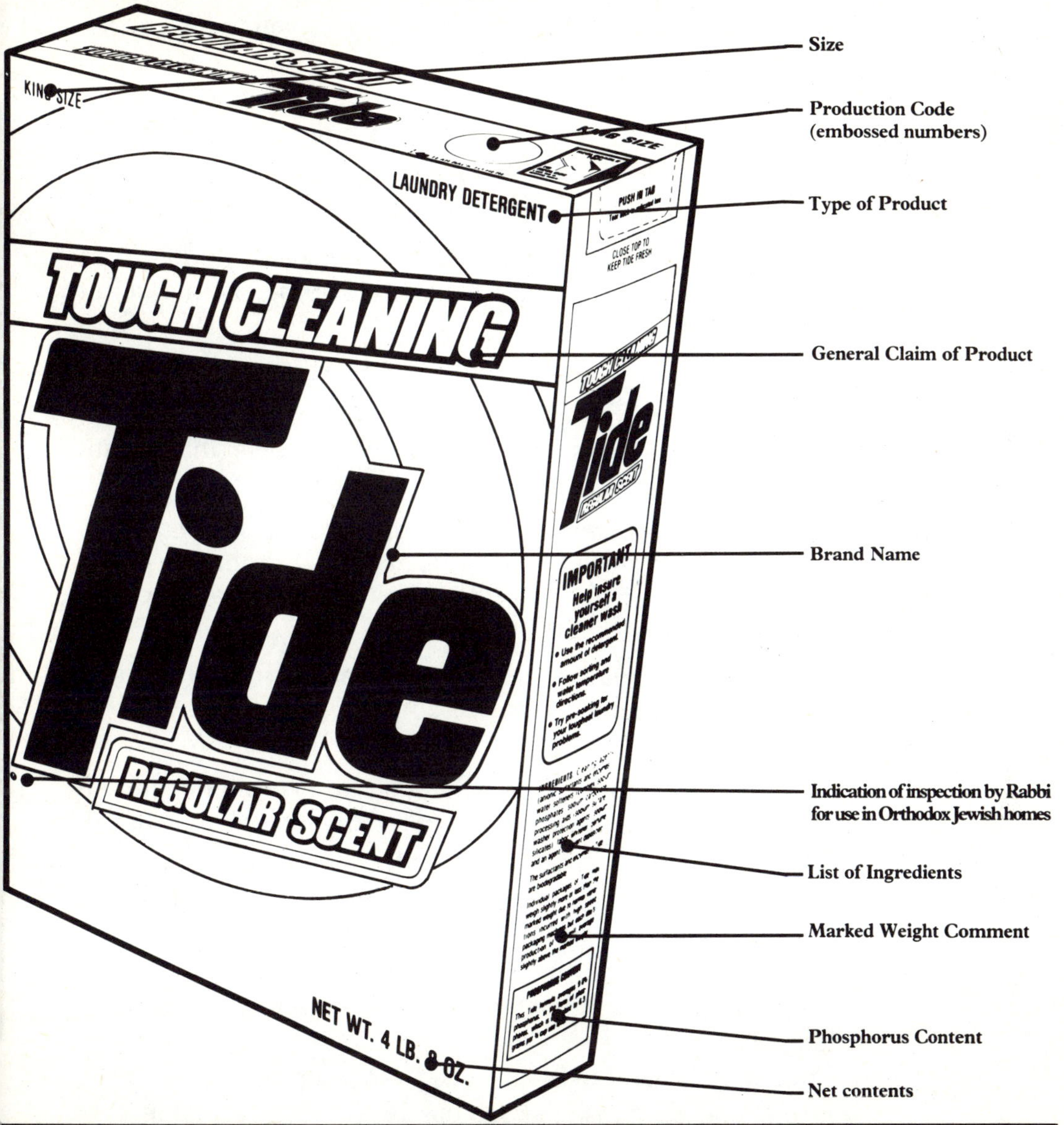
Size
Production Code
(embossed numbers)
Type of Product
General Claim of Product
Brand Name
Indication of inspection by Rabbi
for use in Orthodox Jewish homes
List of Ingredients
Marked Weight Comment
Phosphorus Content
Net contents
KING SIZE
LAUNDRY DETERGENT
TOUGH CLEANING
Tide
REGULAR SCENT
NET WT. 4 LB. 8 OZ.
PUSH IN TAB
CLOSE TOP TO
KEEP TIDE FRESH
IMPORTANT
Help insure
yourself a
cleaner wash

TO SPECIFIC PROCTER & GAMBLE PRODUCTS

EPA Numbers

Registration Number

Indicates the claims for disinfecting have been approved by the U.S. Environmental Protection Agency.

Example: Comet Cleanser
EPA Reg. No. 3573-37

Establishment Number

Indicates location of plant where product was made.

Example: Comet Cleanser EPA Est. No. 3573-NY-1

Caution and First Aid Statement

"If swallowed, give a glassful of water or milk. Call a physician. In case of eye contact, flush with water. Keep product out of reach of children." Example: Cascade package.

Information where product should not be used

Example: Comet Cleanser "Not recommended for use on silver."

Indication of inspection by Rabbi for use in Orthodox Jewish homes during Passover.

Example: Cascade package "P"

again. So when I store the product, I must make certain nothing happens to damage its quality.

Just a few simple guidelines will protect your investment:

> *When I store the product, I must make certain nothing happens to damage its quality.*

- Look for storage instructions on the label, and follow them to the letter. Don't experiment—the experts who wrote the instructions have tried everything.
- Store products in a cool, dry place.
- Do not put a product box in a damp place or puddle. The package may be moisture-resistant to some extent but not water-proof.
- Follow directions for opening the package.
- Close the package tightly after use. This protects the product from dampness, light, or anything else that might damage the product. Prevents messy spills, too.
- Do not store cleaning or laundry products in cabinets where food is stored. Accidents happen. Somebody might confuse one of these products with a food package and swallow the wrong thing.
- For the same reason, do not remove cleaning or laundry products from their original containers and put them in packages that food came in.
- If a product is flammable, obviously you would not store it near a range, furnace, water heater, or anywhere close to a flame.
- Of course you would also always store these products out of the reach of children and pets.

Now that you've chosen your product, used it, stored what is left, what next?

You may be tempted—go ahead!—to step back and admire yourself, and perhaps find somebody to talk everything over with: How the product worked, whether results measured up to expectations, maybe a question or two that stuck in your mind as you went along. You will be happy to know somebody is waiting for your call.

2/How to Choose the Right Product

Take Your Questions to the Manufacturer

One of the most helpful developments in recent years is the rapid growth of what manufacturers call their Consumer Information Services. These are staffed by people who have expert knowledge about a company's product areas, and are available to answer any question. Look on the product package and you will find an address to which you can write. Procter & Gamble also lists a toll-free 800-line number (see box, Page 20) on each package.

Consumer Services is a two-way proposition: you get the answer to almost any product question that is on your mind, and the manufacturer gets a better understanding of the problems you have and the types of products you need.

There is no limit to your product questions. Here are a few possibilities to get you started:

- Ask advice about choosing a product for a particular problem. (Be prepared to describe the nature of your cleaning problem in detail, and the appliances or equipment you use.)
- Ask for an explanation on how to use a product in a bit more detail than the package directions carry.
- Ask for more details about the product ingredients or other features.
- Point out product features you especially like, or speak your mind freely if you would like to see something added to the product.

You will find a phone call or letter very productive. Here is a little tip: Get all your facts together before you call or write.

If you have a problem with a consumer product, be prepared to give the following information (the diagram of a Tide

Consumer Services is a two-way proposition: you get the answer to almost any product question that is on your mind, and the manufacturer gets a better understanding of the problems you have and the types of products you need.

package on Pages 16-17 may be helpful in pointing out where some of these and other details on the package are found):

— the brand name

— exact size of package

— product type or package description

— Manufacturer's Code (for P&G products the Production Code and TASCC Code)

— date of purchase, the name and address of the store where you bought it.

Then tell Consumer Services exactly when and how you used the product and what happened. Provide any other facts that might be helpful.

If you are writing, don't forget to spell out the company name and mailing address on the envelope. And be sure to include your own name, mailing address and phone number (including area code).

Consumer Services' sole purpose is to help you, so don't be timid. Fire away!

Laundry Products		Cleaning Products	Dishwashing Products
(1-800-543-0485) **DETERGENTS**	**(1-800-543-0485)** **SOAP**	**(1-800-543-1745)** **CLEANERS**	**(1-800-543-0485)** **HAND DISHWASHING**
Bold (1965) Cheer (1950) Dash (1954) Dreft (1933) Era (1972) Gain (1966) Liquid Bold 3 (1985) Liquid Cheer (1986) Liquid Tide (1984) Oxydol (1927) Solo (1979) Tide (1946)	Ivory Snow (1930) **(1-800-543-0485)** **BLEACH** Biz (1957) **(1-800-543-1745)** **FABRIC SOFTENERS** Bounce (1972) Downy (1960)	Mr. Clean (1958) Spic and Span (1945) Spic and Span Pine Liquid (1983) Top Job (1963) **(1-800-543-1745)** **CLEANSERS** Comet (1956) Comet Liquid (1976) Mr. Clean Cleanser (1986)	Dawn (1972) Ivory Liquid (1957) Joy (1949) **(1-800-543-0485)** **AUTOMATIC DISHWASHING** Cascade (1955) Liquid Cascade (1986)
(Year product became available)			

Chapter 2

Related Charts

Chart 2.1   Ingredients in Laundering, Cleaning and Dishwashing Products

Chart 2.2   Product Categories

Ingredients In Laundering, Cleaning and Dishwashing Products

MAJOR INGREDIENTS	TYPES	FUNCTIONS
Builders	*Sequestering* (complex phosphates) excel in their ability to sequester hardness minerals because they hold them tightly in solution. They also chemically react with soils to aid in their removal. *Precipitating* (carbonates, silicates) tie up water hardness minerals, but form an insoluble residue which can sometimes coat washer parts and fabrics. *Ion Exchange* (aluminosilicate) tie up calcium hardness minerals but need an additional builder to control magnesium.	Soften water by tying up water hardness. Increase the efficiency of the surfactant system by helping to prevent water hardness from interfering with the cleaning functions of the surfactant. Provide a desirable level of alkalinity which aids cleaning. Help disperse and suspend soils and prevent them from redepositing on fabrics or surfaces being cleaned. Aid in soil removal.
Surfactants (Cleaning agents)	*Anionics* are widely used, since they are particularly effective at oily soil cleaning and clay soil suspension. They have high sudsing characteristics. *Nonionics* are especially good at removing oily soils. They have low sudsing characteristics. *Cationics* provide detergency, softening and antistatic benefits.	Improve the wetting ability of water. Loosen and remove soils with the aid of mechanical action (washer agitation or manual scrubbing). Emulsify, dissolve or suspend soils.

Chart 2.1

WHERE USED (PRODUCT CATEGORY)

Granular laundry detergents

Some liquid laundry detergents

Automatic dishwashing detergents

Household cleaners

Some liquid laundry detergents use either a combination of surfactants and builders or surfactants alone to produce the desired end result.

GENERAL INFORMATION

Of the three types of builders, sequestering is preferable to precipitating and ion exchanging.

Hand dishwashing liquid detergents do not need builders; instead, they use only specific surfactants to handle the various food soils found in hand dishwashing.

Laundry detergents (granular and liquid)

Dishwashing detergents (hand and automatic)

Household cleaners

Because of their low sudsing characteristics, nonionics are frequently used in automatic dishwashing products, where sudsing can hinder cleaning and in household cleaners, where sudsing makes rinsing difficult.

Nonionics are especially suitable for use in liquid laundry products and hand dishwashing detergents because of their oily soil removal characteristics. Where suds are desirable, anionics are used in combination with nonionic surfactants.

Surfactants are organic compounds consisting of two parts: a water-loving (hydrophilic) portion and a water-hating (hydrophobic) portion. The water-hating ends attach themselves to the soil particles while the water-seeking ends are attracted to the water. The surfactant molecules surround the soil particles, break them up and force them away from the soiled surface, then suspend the soil particles in the wash solution.

To be more effective detergents will contain more than one kind of surfactant since they differ in their ability to remove certain types of soil, in their effectiveness on different surfaces and in their response to water hardness.

The surfactants in all Procter & Gamble products have been biodegradable since July 1, 1965, when the detergent industry voluntarily converted to the use of quickly biodegradable surfactants from the previously used surfactants which degraded slowly.

(Continued)

Ingredients In Laundering, Cleaning and Dishwashing Products *(Continued)*

OTHER INGREDIENTS	TYPES	FUNCTIONS
Abrasive Minerals	Ground silica Feldspar Limestone	Provide the scouring action needed to remove: 1) soil embedded in pits and scratches in household surfaces and 2) cooked-on food in pots and pans. Help reduce the amount of hand rubbing needed to remove soil.
Anti-redeposition Agents	Complex cellulosic materials such as carboxymethylcellulose (CMC) and methylcellulose. Synthetic materials such as polyethylene glycol, polyacrylates and polyethoxylated imines.	Aid in preventing loosened soil from redepositing onto cleaned fabrics.
Chlorine Bleach	Sodium and potassium salts of dichloroisocyanurate and trichloroisocyanuric acid Chlorinated trisodium phosphate Liquid Chlorine	Chemically attacks soils, making them easier to remove. Helps solubilize protein soils, like egg and milk. Decolorizes stains. Disinfects and deodorizes surfaces.
Colorants	Pigments or other coloring material	Lend an individuality to the product. Dramatize a special additive contributing to product performance.
Corrosion Inhibitors	Usually, sodium silicates	Help protect washer and dishwasher parts from corrosion. Help prevent the removal of china patterns washed in the dishwasher.
Enzymes	Protease Amylase	Aid in breaking down complex soils, especially proteins such as grass and blood, so these soils can be more easily removed by other detergent ingredients.

Chart 2.1

WHERE USED (PRODUCT CATEGORY)	GENERAL INFORMATION
Granular and liquid cleansers	
Laundry detergents (granular and liquid)	Light duty liquids designed for hand dishwashing and household cleaners generally do not contain antiredeposition agents.
Automatic dishwashing detergents Some cleansers	All-purpose cleaners, hand dishwashing liquids and laundry detergents seldom contain chlorine bleach.
Laundry detergents (granular and liquid) Dishwashing detergents (hand and automatic dishwashing) Household cleaners	Blue colorants in laundry products may provide a bluing which imparts a desirable blue/white color to white fabrics.
Laundry detergents (granular and liquid) Automatic dishwashing detergents	Light duty liquids designed for hand dishwashing and household cleaners generally do not contain corrosion inhibitors.
Presoak products Some laundry detergents	Especially effective when soaking and/or adding product directly to stain.

(Continued)

Ingredients In Laundering, Cleaning and Dishwashing Products *(Continued)*

OTHER INGREDIENTS	TYPES	FUNCTIONS
Fabric Softening/Static Control Agents	Materials ranging from quaternary ammonium salts to specialty chemicals.	Impart softness and control static electricity in fabrics.
Fluorescent Whitening Agents (FWA's or brighteners)	Complex organic molecules which adhere to fabrics as though they were a dye.	Absorb unseen ultraviolet rays from the sun or fluorescent light sources and convert this energy to visible light to enhance fabric appearance and maintain whiteness or brightness.
Fragrances	A wide range of perfumes ranging from floral to spicy to woodsy to fruity, etc., scents.	Contribute to the character of the product. Cover the chemical odor of the detergent and the odor of soils in the washing solution. Impart a pleasant scent to fabrics. Provide a pleasant impression when the package is opened.
Opacifiers	Vary depending upon the soap/detergent system	Provide a rich, creamy, opaque appearance to the product.
Oxygen Bleach	Sodium perborate tetrahydrate	Provides an all-fabric bleaching action for stain and soil removal.
Processing Aids	There is a considerable list of ingredients in this category. Some examples are: sodium sulfate, water and solvents like alcohol.	Provide the product with the right physical properties for its intended use. For example: Sodium sulfate helps provide crisp, free-flowing granules. Alcohols are often used in liquid products where they serve as solvents for the detergent ingredients, adjust the viscosity and prevent product separation. Since liquids contain water, alcohols also provide protection to the product under extremely cold storage conditions by lowering the freezing point.

Chart 2.1

**WHERE USED
(PRODUCT CATEGORY)**   **GENERAL INFORMATION**

Laundry detergents (granular and liquid)
Liquid and sheet-type fabric softeners

Laundry detergents (granular and liquid)   Household cleaners and hand dishwashing
Laundry aid products, such as presoaks, liquid   liquids do not contain FWA's.
fabric softeners, detergent boosters and oxygen
bleaches

All detergents have some level of fragrance.

Some liquid laundry detergents
Some hand dishwashing detergents
Some all-purpose cleaners

Some granular presoak and laundry products

Laundry detergents (granular and liquid)
Dishwashing products (hand and automatic)
Most household cleaners

(Continued)

27

Ingredients In Laundering, Cleaning and Dishwashing Products *(Continued)*

OTHER INGREDIENTS	TYPES	FUNCTIONS
Special Ingredients	Ammonia compounds Mineral or organic acids Quaternary ammonium salts Sodium hydroxide and others	Used in specific applications where the chemical characteristics are required for specific product attributes.
Suds Control Agents	Suds stabilizers	Suds stabilizers aid in maintaining voluminous suds.
	Suds suppressors	Suds suppressors inhibit sudsing or control it at a low level.

Chart 2.1

**WHERE USED
(PRODUCT CATEGORY)**

GENERAL INFORMATION

Toilet bowl cleaners

Oven and drain cleaners

Suds stabilizers are used in liquid dishwashing products where a high, lasting level of suds is desirable.

Suds suppressors are used in laundry detergents designed for: 1) consumers preferring low sudsing products, 2) suds sensitive automatic washers, 3) all-purpose cleaners to provide easy rinsing and 4) automatic dishwashing detergents.

Product Categories — Chart 2.2

A. LAUNDRY PRODUCTS

Soaps
    Light Duty
    Soap Bars
Detergents
    Heavy Duty
    Light Duty

B. LAUNDRY AIDS

Bleaches
    Chlorine
    Oxygen
Bluings
Detergent Boosters
Fabric Softeners
Presoaks
Pretreat Soil and Stain Removers
Starches, Fabric Finishes and Sizings
Water Softeners

C. DISHWASHING PRODUCTS

Detergents
    Light Duty
    Automatic Dishwashing

D. AUTOMATIC DISHWASHING AIDS

Specialty Products
Rinse Agents

E. HOUSEHOLD CLEANERS

All-purpose Cleaners	**Drain Cleaners**	**Toilet Bowl Cleaners**
Carpet Cleaners	**Glass Cleaners**	**Traditional Cleaners**
Carpet Fresheners	**Insecticides**	**Tub, Tile and Sink Cleaners**
Cleansers	**Metal Cleaners**	**Upholstery Cleaners**
Disinfectants	**Oven Cleaners**	**Waxes and Polishes**

3 How To Organize Your Laundering

The objective is to make the work much easier, get much better results, save time, save money and—who doesn't need this?—give yourself a feeling of genuine accomplishment.

If somebody told you (as this chapter will) that the best way to do your laundry is to follow nine rules, you would probably throw up your hands in horror. "Nine rules! Laundering can't be that hard!"

So here is the good news. The nine rules are simply the way to organize your laundering. The objective is to make the work much easier, get much better results, save time, save money and—who doesn't need this?—give yourself a feeling of genuine accomplishment. (Many people think laundering, done right, is the most satisfying of all household tasks, because nothing beats the smell and touch of freshly cleaned clothes and linens.)

This chapter tells how to organize your laundering. You will also find dozens of tips on how to remove difficult stains and charts describing special problems and solutions.

9 Rules to Good Laundering Results

Let's begin with the nine rules.

The first thing to do is to write them down and attach them to the cleaning closet door or wherever you are likely to see them frequently during the day. The whole idea is to memorize them, so they become second nature. Before long, as experienced homemakers will attest, you will do these things automatically. Notice how simple the nine rules are:

1. Read and follow Care Labels.

2. Sort clothes carefully.

3. Pretreat soiled or stained areas before washing.

4. Choose the right laundry product for the job.

5. Follow the directions on product packages.

6. Use the proper water temperature.

7. Use the proper washing action.

8. Rinse thoroughly.

9. Dry clothes properly (hang/fold/store neatly).

Hardly horrifying, are they? But get into the habit of checking them off before you start your laundering because, as we examine them next in detail, you will see how they can make or break your effort.

Rule 1. Read and Follow Care Labels

Before you buy any garment, read the Care Label. What it tells you may very well determine whether you make the purchase or look for something else.

Before you buy any garment, read the Care Label. What it tells you may very well determine whether you make the purchase or look for something else.

Since the Federal Trade Commission first required Care Labels in 1972, the instructions on these labels have become better and better at answering questions that trouble consumers.

For example, every clothing item must have either laundering or drycleaning instructions. If the garment can be laundered, the label must say whether it can be done by hand or machine, water temperature restrictions and recommended drying and ironing procedures.

If the garment cannot tolerate a specific laundering practice, the Care Label must contain a warning such as "Do not,"

"No," or "Only." For example, "Do not use chlorine bleach," or "Only non-chlorine bleach, when needed."

Suppose the label carries no restrictions. Then use any laundering and drying method. "Machine wash, tumble dry" means you can use hot, warm or cold water, any washer cycle, any drying temperature.

One reason the labels are required to be so complete and specific is this: Clothing items may look almost exactly alike, but need very different care. It's a good idea to compare baby clothes, sweatshirts, jeans, everything. One baby blanket may have a "No bleach" label, another may not. So when you go shopping, ask yourself: "Can I wash this garment with other items—or do I need a separate load?" If it is an extra load, there goes extra time, effort and the cost of more laundry product.

Also when shopping, consider whether a garment will receive heavy soiling during wear. If so, do the care instructions allow you to use washing procedures necessary to remove the soil, i.e., hot water, bleach, detergent, regular agitation in the washer?

Now take six or seven minutes and read Chart 3.1 (Apparel Care Labeling Guide), Pages 47-49. It will help you understand the shades of difference between various labels, and realize how explicit and helpful these labels are.

Two other charts serve as further guides: Chart 3.2 (Fiber Facts) Pages 50-59 summarizes the major man-made and natural textile fibers, their generic and trade names, uses, characteristics and miscellaneous general information regarding their care. Special Laundering Instructions are listed on Chart 3.3, Pages 60-77.

Rule 2. Sort Clothes Carefully

Sorting is a key step in laundering and also in soaking clothes before the actual washing. The people who make the clothes, the cleaning products and the washing machines have learned, through rigorous testing, that careless sorting can mess up the whole laundering process.

Sorting is a key step in laundering and also in soaking clothes before the actual washing.

Proper sorting is as easy as it is sensible, if you follow a few guidelines.

- Sort by color. This means separate loads for:

    1. whites, solid pastels and light prints
    2. medium and bright colors
    3. dark colors

    (When you buy new colored items, it is a good idea to wash them separately to see whether they are colorfast, i.e., won't fade or run, before putting them in the washer with other clothes.)

- Sort by fabric and garment construction. Separate loosely-knit or woven fabrics, very sheer and delicate fabrics and garments with unfinished and narrow seams. These require gentle agitation or a short wash time. Wash them alone or with similar items.
  Remember to separate lint-producing fabrics such as terry cloth robes, towels and chenille spreads, and wash them with similar items. You'll save yourself a plague of headaches.

- Sort by the kind and amount of soil in the clothes. Separate the heavily soiled items—mud, oily and greasy stains—because these require their own kind of treatment.

- And sort by size of item. It is a good idea to mix large and small items because together they produce the best washing action.

While sorting, get into the habit of doing these little things, if you want to save yourself from jangling nerves later:

- Close all zippers, hooks and other devices.
- Turn pockets inside out and brush away lint and crumbs. This helps prevent stains. It also reminds you to remove pencils, crayons, coins, toys, tissues and other little missiles that collect in pockets and can create problems.
- Tie sashes and buckle washable belts so they won't tangle or tear during the washing action.

3/How to Organize Your Laundering

- Mend rips, tears and loose hems before putting them in the wash—otherwise the agitation might do serious damage.
- Plan wash loads to make good use of water, cleaning products and electricity, but not so big that items can't move freely in the wash water. Items must move easily and turn over (disappear and re-appear) in the wash solution to provide good uniform cleaning results.

Rule 3. Pretreat Soiled or Stained Areas before Washing

Sometimes you wonder whether anything in the world is as stubborn as a stain that won't come out. There are a thousand kinds of stains, and every one of them can drive you to distraction. But there is hope, as you will see in a moment.

Chart 3.4 (Products for Pretreating or Removing Stains) offers a starting point, Page 79. Basically, depending on the soil or stain and the fabric, there are three procedures you can follow:

- *Soak.* This can be done in a basin, laundry sink or washer, using a solution of laundry detergent. If the problem is to remove protein and starch-based stains, try a detergent or laundry aid product containing enzymes. Soak large loads in a washer, using the automatic soak cycle or operating the controls by hand. Soaking can be done in 30 minutes. If the problem is severe, soak overnight in a plastic pail or laundry tub. Then wash with fresh water and detergent.
- *Prewash.* This can be done by hand in a basin, laundry sink or washer. Some washers have an automatic prewash cycle, others have to be operated manually. It is always smart to follow the washer manufacturer's instructions. Use a laundry detergent or, for very heavy soil, use a prewash product along with a laundry detergent. Follow this with a regular machine wash and the recommended amount of laundry detergent.

- *Pretreat.* This means treating spots and stains before laundering, and sometimes removing them completely. Rub the stain with bar soap, or liquid detergent, or a paste of water and granular detergent. Or use a pretreat soil and stain remover.

Acting immediately is very important in removing stains.

Then there is the matter of how to remove stains caused by such things as rust, ballpoint pens or candle wax. These are truly difficult stains requiring special products and treatments. Fortunately, experts have clinically examined dozens of individual stains and advised how to deal with them. We will come to them in a minute or so. You will probably make as much use of this list as anything in this book—so always have the book handy to consult when a stain occurs. Acting immediately is very important in removing stains.

Here are a few tips:

- Treat stains as soon as possible. Obviously, it is easier to remove stains while they are fresh. Take non-washables to the drycleaner as soon as possible and tell what caused the stain.

- Always test any stain remover on a sample of fabric taken from a seam allowance, a facing or a hidden part of the garment. Apply the amount of product recommended on the package, allowing it to stand on the fabric sample for the recommended amount of time. Then rinse. This will tell you how the product affects the color and texture of the fabric. If anything goes wrong, you have the wrong product, and this test will save the garment.

- When treating a spot, place it face down on paper towels and apply the stain remover to the backside of the stain. This will help push the stain off the surface. If you apply the remover to the face of the stain, you force the stain into the fabric.

- When using a bleach product, bleach the entire garment, not just the stain area. (Also bleach any separate but matching items which are washable, i.e., belt.) This prevents odd discolorations or patches of color change. And if the garment is lightened during bleaching, the color change will be uniform.

3/How to Organize Your Laundering

- If you use chlorine bleach with detergents containing enzymes, add the bleach about halfway through the wash for best results.

It is always very important to read the instructions on bleach packages. For example:

Chlorine bleach: Use with bleachable fabrics such as white and colorfast cotton, linen, polyester, acrylic, triacetate, some nylon, rayon, blends of these fabrics, and permanent press.

Oxygen bleach: *Use with most washable fabrics*

- Air dry articles to check for stain removal (dryer drying could make the stain more difficult to remove).
- Always launder immediately after removing a stain. This washes away the stain and the stain removal product.

The list of stains and how to deal with them is on Chart 3.5 (Stain Removal Guide) Pages 80-85.

Rule 4. Choose the Right Laundry Product for the Job

If you needed further convincing that choosing the right product is all-important, the list of stains you have just read must have supplied evidence galore. Nothing works with the wrong product.

Chart 3.6 (Laundry Products and Aids) Pages 86-95 helps you see the differences in products so you can make the right choices. It classifies laundry products as soaps, detergents and laundry aids; tells the best way to use them; offers some tips about what these products can and can't do.

Rule 5. Follow the Directions on Product Packages

What do you think is the most common mistake in home laundering?

Many experts believe it is the simplest and most unnecessary mistake of all—using too little of the cleaning product. Make this mistake, and you will surely pay for the error—yellowing, grayness, dullness, streaks and all the other telltale signs that something has gone wrong.

Such a mistake is unnecessary because the manufacturers have tested thoroughly to determine which amounts, under different conditions, should be used to produce the good results you always anticipate.

That is why manufacturers take such painstaking care in writing the directions for the package. (As mentioned earlier, the last thing they want is for you to use the wrong amount and then blame the results on the product.)

Obviously, the best advice is this: Read the package directions and follow them explicitly.

Here is another tip. If you switch from one brand to another, remember each brand is different, so the amount needed may also be different. A concentrated laundry detergent may call for one-fourth of a cup, while a granulated product may require a full cup to do the same job.

The instructions are based on the average washing conditions: a 5-7 pound load of clothes; average soil; moderate water hardness (3.6-7.0 grains per gallon); average water volume (17 gallons for a top-loading washer, 8 gallons for a front-loading washer); regular agitation.

But sometimes conditions are not quite average. Then you must use your own good judgment.

Use more detergent if:

- clothes are exceptionally dirty.
- it's a large load.
- the water is very hard. (For information on water hardness

> **Obviously, the best advice is this: Read the package directions and follow them explicitly.**

3/How to Organize Your Laundering

in your area, consult the local water company or the County Extension Office, listed under U.S. Department of Agriculture in your phone book.)

- the washer is a large capacity and is set to use the extra amount of water.
- the wash action or wash time is reduced to protect delicate items.
- the wash water temperature is set for "warm" or "cold."

Use slightly less detergent if:

- the water is soft.
- the clothes are lightly soiled.
- the load is small.
- a partial water fill is used in the washer.

Since accuracy is so important, use a standard measuring cup. Keep it with your laundry equipment and use it only for detergents. If you must use it for bleach, fabric softeners or other products, rinse it thoroughly after each use.

Rule 6. Use the Proper Water Temperature

Water temperature affects cleaning, wrinkling, stability of non-fast colors and the durability of the fabric.

The Care Label on the garment tells you what water temperature to use if other than hot is recommended. What it doesn't tell you is that water temperature affects cleaning, wrinkling, stability of non-fast colors and the durability of the fabric. Here are the facts.

- *Hot Water* (130°Fahrenheit/54°Centigrade). Hot water does the quickest and best job of cleaning and sanitizing, but it is not suitable for all items. It is best for sturdy whites, colorfast items, diapers and heavily-soiled permanent press fabrics.

41

- *Warm Water* (90°-100°Fahrenheit/32°-38°Centigrade). With warm instead of hot water, there is less chance of washing out color or damaging fabric finishes. Warm water minimizes wrinkling permanent press fabrics and reduces shrinkage of knits. Use it for moderately soiled clothes, colored fabrics that are not colorfast, silks, woolens, permanent press, nylon, acrylic and other man-made fiber fabrics and blends.

- *Cold Water* (Up to 80° Fahrenheit/27° Centigrade approximately.) Cold water minimizes wrinkling and fading of colors, but it does not clean as well as hot or warm water. Use it for washing extra-sensitive colors, very lightly-soiled clothes and items that are not shrink-resistant.

Cold water is excellent for rinsing all loads including those washed in hot or warm water.

Cold water is excellent for rinsing all loads including those washed in hot or warm water.

Rule 7. Use the Proper Washing Action

Most washers offer more than one speed of agitation—"regular or normal" for sturdy items, "slow or gentle" for delicate loads.

Some agitation is necessary for cleaning. The problem is too much agitation can fray the seams of delicate or poorly constructed items, and tears or pulls can occur.

So get in the habit of sorting clothes with the washing action in mind.

Rule 8. Rinse Thoroughly

Rinsing probably doesn't get the attention it deserves. A good way to understand it is this: Washing loosens the dirt, rinsing gets rid of it. It also removes the laundry products, suds and lint. It isn't too hard to imagine what kind of wash you would end up with if the rinsing wasn't properly done. (Your automatic washer usually does this good rinsing job for you.)

Cold water does a good job of rinsing in addition to saving energy. Remember that point, whether you are rinsing by hand or machine.

Rule 9. Dry Clothes Properly (Hang/Fold/Store Neatly)

Look for the Care Label and follow the instructions to the letter. The label will say whether the garment can be dried in an automatic dryer, outdoors or indoors on a line, or flat.

If an automatic dryer is required, watch for two things. One, use the correct drying temperature. Two, remove immediately when the drying time is up. It is important not to overdo the drying because that could cause wrinkling which means extra touch-up pressing for permanent press garments.

Finally, once clothes are clean and ready to wear, complete the job by hanging them up properly or folding them neatly.

How to Launder by Hand

For one reason or another, you may find yourself doing your laundry by hand. Obviously, it is different from the machine laundering just described, but still there are many similarities. The basics always apply.

For hand laundering, start by reading the garment Care Label. It will explain which washing and drying methods are best for the garment.

Next, prepare the solution. It is a good practice to measure the amount of water and follow this formula: For every gallon of water, use one long squirt of a light-duty liquid detergent such as Dawn, Ivory Liquid or Joy. Or, if you prefer, use 1/4 cup of a granular all-purpose detergent such as Tide, Cheer, Oxydol, or Dreft.

Swish the water to disperse the liquid detergent or dissolve the granules.

Then sort the clothes by color, fabric, or other characteristics and wash similar items together, remembering:

- Do a few items at a time. You will do a better washing job because fewer items are easier to handle and clean thoroughly.
- Items that lose dye or color should be washed separately.

Squeeze the washing solution through the clothes. The clothes will rub together somewhat as you do this, and rubbing helps the cleaning process. But, take care, hard rubbing can damage clothes that are not sturdy.

When you are through washing, give the clothes a thorough rinsing in cold water. Rinsing gets rid of the loosened soil and the washing solution, and prevents them from settling back on the clean clothes. Check the Care Label for advice about water removal because some garments should not be twisted, stretched or rung out.

The label will also tell you how to dry the garments—hung on a line or rack, or flat.

Identify Your Laundering Problems

Whatever your laundering problems, you will probably find them listed and solved on Chart 3.7 (Laundering Problems . . . Causes, Solutions, Preventive Measures) Pages 96-105. As you read the chart, circle any particularly difficult or common problem for quick future reference.

Chapter 3

Related Charts

Chart 3.1 Apparel Care Labeling Guide
Chart 3.2 Fiber Facts
Chart 3.3 Special Laundering Instructions
Chart 3.4 Products for Pretreating or Removing Stains
Chart 3.5 Stain Removal Guide for Washable Items
Chart 3.6 Laundry Products and Aids
Chart 3.7 Laundering Problems . . . Causes, Solutions, Preventive Measures

Apparel Care Labeling Guide — Chart 3.1

This guide, based on the Federal Trade Commission Rule 16 CFR 423 as amended effective January 2, 1984, further defines the care instructions found on apparel labels. Additional information from Procter & Gamble and the FTC has been included for clarification.

The Care Label law requires only one cleaning procedure (washing or drycleaning) to be specified.

Be Sure To Read All Care Instructions Completely

When label reads: / *It means:*

	When label reads:	It means:
Alternate Cleaning Procedures	Machine Wash	Wash by any customary machine method including commercial laundering.
	Hand Wash	Launder only by hand.
	Do Not Have Commercially Laundered	Use only laundering methods/equipment designed for residential use or use in self-service establishments.
	Dryclean	May be drycleaned by normal method or in coin operated drycleaning machine.
	No Label Statement Concerning Drycleaning	Drycleaner and consumer accept responsibility if garment is drycleaned unsuccessfully.
	Professionally Dryclean	Included with this term may be other instructions to be followed by your professional drycleaner.
Water Temperature Statement	Machine Wash (No temperature statement)	Any water temperature including hot up to 150°F (66°C), can be regularly used. Hot water provides best cleaning.
	Machine Wash Warm or Hand Wash Warm	Use warm water, 90°F to 110°F (32° to 43°C), which is hand comfortable or warm machine setting.
	Machine Wash Cold or Hand Wash Cold	Use cold water, up to 85°F (29°C), or cold machine setting.

(Continued)

47

Apparel Care Labeling Guide *(Continued)*

	When label reads:	It means:
Bleach Statement	No Label Statement	All bleaches may be used.
	Bleach When Needed	All bleaches may be used when needed.
	Only Non-Chlorine Bleach When Needed	Only non-chlorine bleach may be used when necessary. Chlorine bleach may not be used.
	No Bleach or Do Not Bleach	No bleaches may be used.
Machine Cycle Statement	No Label Statement	Regular/Normal Cycle with regular agitation and spin speed may be used.
	Permanent/Durable Press Cycle	Use appropriate washer setting which has a cooldown or cold spray before the reduced spin.
	Delicate/Gentle Cycle	Use appropriate washer setting (slow agitation and/or reduced wash time).
Special Washing/Handling Statement	No Label Statement	No special washing/handling procedures are necessary.
	No Spin	Remove wash load before the final spin.
	With Like Colors	Wash with colors of similar hue and intensity.
	Separately	Wash alone.
	No Wring or Twist	Do not wring by hand or use rollers on wringer washer. Hang dry, drip dry or dry flat.
	Damp Wipe Only	Clean surface with damp cloth or sponge.

Chart 3.1

When label reads:	It means:
Drying Statement	
Tumble Dry (No temperature statement)	Machine dry. Any temperature setting including hot may be regularly used.
Tumble Dry Medium	Set dryer at medium heat.
Tumble Dry Low	Set dryer at low heat.
Permanent/Durable Press Cycle	Use Permanent/Durable Press Cycle setting.
No Heat	Set dryer to operate without heat or dry flat away from heat.
Remove Promptly	Tumble dry and remove immediately to prevent wrinkling.
Drip Dry	Hang wet on plastic hanger and allow to dry with hand shaping only.
Line Dry	Hang damp from line or bar and allow to dry.
Dry Flat	Lay garment on flat surface.
Block to Dry	Reshape to original size while drying.
Ironing, Pressing Statement	
No Label Statement	Pressing is not needed on a regular basis to preserve the appearance of the garment. Hot iron is safe to use if pressing is occasionally needed.
Iron (No temperature statement)	Ironing is needed. The highest temperature setting may be regularly used.
Warm Iron	Use Medium temperature setting.
Cool Iron	Use lowest temperature setting.
Do not Iron	Do not iron or press with heat.
Steam Iron	Iron or press with steam.
Iron Damp	Dampen garment before ironing.
Use Press Cloth	Use a dry or damp cloth between iron and fabric.

Fiber Facts

The Textile Fiber Products Identification Act as amended in 1969, requires mandatory fiber content labeling in order of predominance by weight for all fibers making up more than 5% of the fabric. The generic name of the fiber must be used, but manufacturers can add the trade name of their fiber.

FIBER TYPE	GENERIC NAME	SOME TRADEMARK NAMES	END USES
Man-made—Cellulosic	Acetate	Ariloft Avron Celanese Chromspun Estron Loftura	Apparel—light and medium weight Drapery and upholstery fabrics Quilted—comforters, mattress pads, jackets
	Rayon (conventional)	Beau-Grip Coloray Enkrome	Apparel—light and medium weight Drapery and upholstery fabric
	Rayon (high wet modulus)	Avril Durvil Zantrel	Apparel (blouses, coats, dresses, lingerie, sportswear, suits, ties) Home furnishings (draperies, bedspreads, sheets, slipcovers, tablecloths, upholstery)
	Triacetate	Arnel	Apparel—dresses, skirts, sportswear Pleated apparel

Chart 3.2

Follow laundering instructions on the Care Label, keeping in mind some soils/stains may need additional treatment to be removed.

This chart summarizes the major man-made and natural textile fibers, their generic and trade names, end uses, characteristics and miscellaneous general information.

CHARACTERISTICS	GENERAL INFORMATION
Drapes well Luxurious feel and luster Economical Poor abrasion resistance Heat sensitive Low wet strength	Can lose body during laundering. Exhibits poor colorfastness when wet. Avoid soaking and hot water washes. Rubbing may damage. Using gentle wash conditions helps minimize fabric abrasion. Use fabric softener to reduce static cling.
Absorbent Moderately durable Wrinkles easily Low wet strength	Rayon has the tendency to lose body, shrink or stretch when wet. Some rayons may need to be drycleaned. Follow care label instructions precisely.
Highly absorbent Soft and comfortable Versatile Good drapability Easy to dye	Maintains fabric body and color better than conventional rayon. Responds well when washed. When pressing, use a moderately hot iron on the wrong side or use a press cloth.
Shrink resistant Wrinkle resistant Retains pleats and crisp finish Tolerates high temperatures Stronger fabric than acetate	More colorfast and less prone to shrinkage than acetate.

(Continued)

Fiber Facts (Continued)

FIBER TYPE	GENERIC NAME	SOME TRADEMARK NAMES	END USES
Man-made—Non-Cellulosic	Acrylic	Acrilan Creslan Orlon Zefran Zefkrome	Knitted apparel (fleecewear, sweaters, outerwear, hosiery) Bathrobes and nightwear Upholstery, draperies Blankets
	Aramid	Nomex Kevlar	Protective apparel for firefighters and others in hazardous occupations Bullet proof vests → Industrial applications only
	Glass	Fiberglas	Draperies
	Modacrylic	SEF	Children's sleepwear Blankets Draperies

Chart 3.2

CHARACTERISTICS	GENERAL INFORMATION
Soft, warm bulking properties resembling wool Good wrinkle resistance and crease recovery Moderate abrasion resistance Heat sensitive May pill in some yarn constructions Moth resistant	Easily cleaned, but oily stains need pretreatment before washing. Some acrylics lose resiliency and stretch with wear. Some acrylics need tumble drying to maintain garment size. Use fabric softener to reduce static cling. When pressing, use steam or warm (not hot) iron.
Highly flame-resistant Does not melt Extremely strong fiber	Good performer. Do not use chlorine bleach.
Flame resistant Weather and sun resistant Does not absorb moisture Excellent wrinkle resistant Low abrasion resistance Seam and yarn slippage may occur in some constructions	Glass fibers are easily damaged by mechanical action. Curtains blowing in and out of a window or rubbing against a sill can produce holes in the fabric. Avoid direct pretreatment/scrubbing because color may be removed. Most glass fabrics are not machine washable or dryable. Small glass fibers remaining in a washer may be deposited in the fabrics of the next wash load causing minor to severe skin irritation when items are worn. (See Special Laundering Instructions, Pages 60–77.)
Inherent flame resistance Other characteristics are similar to acrylics	More heat sensitive than acrylic. May pill excessively.

(Continued)

Fiber Facts *(Continued)*

FIBER TYPE	GENERIC NAME	SOME TRADEMARK NAMES	END USES
Man-made Non-Cellulosic (Continued)	Nylon	Anso Antron Blue "C" Cantrece Caprolan Enkalure Enkasheer Multisheer Shareen Zefran	Blouses, dresses, foundation garments, hosiery, lingerie, raincoats, ski/snow apparel, windbreakers Bedspreads, draperies, curtains, upholstery
	Olefin	Herculon Marquesa Lana Patlon	Knitted sportswear Sweaters Slipcovers Upholstery Underwear Pantyhose Protective work clothing
	Polyester	Avlin Caprolan Dacron Encron Fortrel Kodel Trivira	Blouses, shirts, dresses, slacks, suits, lingerie Often combined with other fibers for permanent press apparel, tablecloths, sheets, curtains, draperies. Fiberfill
	Rubber	—	Foundation garments Bras Rain coats Rug backing Rubber coated apparel and sportswear

Chart 3.2

CHARACTERISTICS	GENERAL INFORMATION
Exceptionally strong High abrasion resistance Low moisture absorbency Retains permanent shape	Nylon readily picks up dye from colored items in the wash water. This transferred color may be permanent. To help prevent dye transfer, wash white nylon separately from colored items. Hot water washing with detergent and chlorine bleach will generally improve cleaning of white nylon. Test bleachability first, since chlorine bleach may destroy the surface applied whitening agents on some nylon. Rinse with cold water to minimize wrinkling and use fabric softener to reduce static cling.
Soil resistant Abrasion resistant Sensitive to heat Quick drying Very light weight Good insulator	Tends to float in wash water. Placing items in a mesh bag helps keep them submerged for better cleaning. Olefin's sensitivity to heat requires very low heat drying. Rinse in cold water to minimize wrinkling and use fabric softener to reduce static cling.
Strong Resistant to stretching and shrinking Wrinkle resistant May pill when abraded Attracts and holds on to oily soil	Polyester's affinity for oily soils requires special attention prior to washing. Pretreat stained areas by: 1) rubbing in undiluted liquid detergent or a paste made with granular detergent and water, or 2) applying a spray-type pretreatment product. Excellent colorfastness, allows the use of chlorine bleach with detergent to improve cleaning and stain removal. Rinse in cold water to minimize wrinkling and use fabric softener to reduce static cling.
Good stretch and recovery	Can be damaged by oils, including body oils, sunlight, high heat and perspiration. In some rubber coated fabrics, bondings may become soft and tacky. To minimize this problem, use detergents containing only anionic surfactants, line dry and avoid using solvent based pretreatment products.

(Continued)

Fiber Facts *(Continued)*

FIBER TYPE	GENERIC NAME	SOME TRADEMARK NAMES	END USES
Man-made Non-Cellulosic (Continued)	Spandex	Lycra Glospan Numa	Athletic apparel Bathing suits Stretch lace Foundation garments Slacks Support and surgical hose
Natural	Cotton	—	Blouses, dresses, shirts, sportswear, underwear, diapers Towels, curtains Often used in blends with polyester
	Linen	—	Blouses Dresses Suits Table linens
	Ramie	—	Knitted sweaters Trousers Blouses Sportswear

Chart 3.2

CHARACTERISTICS	GENERAL INFORMATION
High degree of stretch and recovery Abrasion resistant Lightweight Tends to yellow with time	Some spandex can be bleached with chlorine bleach; for other types of spandex, use an oxygen bleach along with the detergent.
Absorbent, durable, versatile Wrinkles easily Comfortable Will shrink, unless treated to resist shrinkage	Many brightly colored cottons in today's market have dyes that will bleed in wash water or rub off during wear. To help control dye loss, wash separately and pretreat stains without rubbing. To produce good fabric appearance with a minimum of care, cotton usually needs to be treated with a wrinkle resistant finish and blended with polyester.
Beauty and luster endure through frequent launderings Very absorbent Does not shed lint Wrinkles easily unless treated to resist wrinkling	Usually blended with other fabrics in today's garments.
Very absorbent Wrinkles easily Strong durable fiber	Generally used in blends with rayon, polyester, cotton, etc.

(Continued)

Fiber Facts (Continued)

FIBER TYPE	GENERIC NAME	SOME TRADEMARK NAMES	END USES
Natural (Continued)	Silk	—	Blouses Dresses Suits Scarfs
	Wool	—	Sweaters Socks Sportswear Dresses Suits Blankets

Chart 3.2

CHARACTERISTICS

Natural luster
Luxurious soft feel
Drapes well
Moderately wrinkle resistant
Absorbent
Comfortable to wear

GENERAL INFORMATION

Silk is damaged by chlorine bleach.

Many dyes are affected by sunlight and perspiration. Wearing dress shields will help prevent underarm discoloration from perspiration.

Using a neutral pH hand dishwashing detergent, like Ivory Liquid, will help minimize color change of bright acid dyes, commonly used on silk.

Some silk dyes bleed during laundering, thus should be laundered separately.

Some fabrics water spot readily or produce a ring mark when treated with a solvent on soiled surface.

Avoid excessive rubbing when pretreating spots/stains to help prevent color loss.

Use fabric softener to reduce static cling.

Warm and comfortable
Sheds wrinkles well
Very absorbent
Resilient and elastic
Naturally water-repellent and flame resistant

Wool is damaged by chlorine bleach.

Prolonged soaking may damage light/medium colors.

Excessive rubbing, abrasion or washing agitation causes felting and/or shrinkage. For untreated wool, agitation should be limited to a maximum of two minutes for washing and one minute for rinsing.

Using a neutral pH hand dishwashing detergent, like Ivory Liquid, will help minimize the color change of acid dyes commonly used on wools.

Special Laundering Instructions

ITEM	LAUNDERING PROCEDURE
Baby Clothes/Diapers	BABY CLOTHES Follow care instructions on the label. If not available consider the following: To Wash: Prior to washing, pretreat soils/stains (see procedures for "Heavy Soil"). Launder using a laundry detergent, warm (100°F) water (use hot, 130°F, water if heavily soiled) and the Regular Cycle if items are sturdily constructed. If fragilely constructed, use the Delicate Cycle (see procedures for "Delicate Fabrics"). To Dry: Dryer dry or line dry. DIAPERS Rinse soiled diapers immediately in cold water. To Wash: Limit wash load to no more than 3 dozen diapers. Wash separately from baby clothes, bedding, etc., using hot (130°F) water, detergent and chlorine bleach. Follow package instructions for recommended amounts of detergent and bleach. To Dry: Dryer dry or line dry.
Bathroom Carpeting, Throw Rugs, etc.	Follow care instructions on the label. If not available, consider the following: Shake or vacuum loose dirt and pretreat spots/stains before washing (see procedures for "Heavy Soil"). To Wash: Use the Regular Cycle, a granular laundry detergent and warm (100°F) wash water (use hot, 130°F water if heavily soiled). To Dry: Dryer dry. Hang and air dry if rugs have rubber or foam backing.

Chart 3.3

ADDITIONAL INFORMATION

BABY CLOTHES
Be aware some Care Label instructions may not be adequate for removal of some baby soils. The kinds of cleaning procedures (hot water, chlorine bleach, soaks) usually needed to clean baby soils may not be compatible with the colorfastness of dyes. Read Care Labels prior to purchase so baby items can be properly cleaned.

Use a fabric softener to improve clothing comfort.

DIAPERS
While accumulating a wash load of diapers, soak in a plastic pail using cold water, 2 tablespoons laundry detergent and 2 tablespoons chlorine bleach per gallon of water. When preparing to wash, empty pail into automatic washer and spin excess water from diapers.

Wash separately because of potential linting and instability of dye.

When washing one or two small rugs, the addition of bath towels may be necessary to keep the wash load balanced.

(Continued)

Special Laundering Instructions *(Continued)*

ITEM	LAUNDERING PROCEDURE
Bedspreads, Comforters	Follow care instructions on the label. If not available, consider the following for washable spreads/comforters: Pretreat spots/stains before washing (see procedures for "Heavy Soil"). <u>To Wash</u>: Wash separately using the Regular Cycle and warm (100°F) water. Add the laundry detergent to the washer first, then the item, making sure it is submerged around the agitator. <u>To Dry</u>: Dryer dry or hang over two parallel lines and straighten to shape.
Blankets and Woolens (For laundering Synthetic Blankets, see Permanent Press)	Follow care instructions on the label. If not available consider the following: Pretreat spots/stains before washing (see procedures for "Heavy Soil"). <u>To Wash</u>: Add laundry detergent to washer first, then fill with warm (100°F) water and agitate. Stop washer and add the woolens or unfolded blanket, submerging the load evenly around the agitator. Soak 10 to 15 minutes. Gently agitate for 1 minute. (Too much agitation will shrink/felt woolens.) Manually advance the timer to drain and spin for about 1 minute with normal speed. <u>To Rinse</u>: Fill washer again and add fabric softener. Agitate for 1 minute. Spin out water. <u>To Dry</u>: Hang woolen blanket over two parallel lines, straighten to shape. When partially dry, change position and straighten again. Brush up nap with a nylon brush, when dry. Lay woolen garments flat on premeasured patterns and gently block to original measurements.

Chart 3.3

ADDITIONAL INFORMATION

Do not wash cotton-filled comforters unless they are quilted or stitched; cotton batting, when only tucked, tends to slip and become lumpy.

Before washing, measure or trace the outline of woolen garments on clean white paper. Use these patterns for drying and blocking garments to prewashed size. Save patterns for future washings.

(Continued)

Special Laundering Instructions *(Continued)*

ITEM	LAUNDERING PROCEDURE
Cleaning Cloths	To Wash: Use hot (130°F) water and the Regular Cycle with a laundry detergent and a chlorine bleach—using the amount recommended for heavy soil. To Dry: Tumble dry with high heat or line dry.
Curtains, Draperies	Follow care instructions on the label. If not available consider the following: To Wash: Use warm (100°F) water, a laundry liquid or dissolved granular detergent and the Gentle Cycle. For heavily soiled washable curtains/draperies, soak 5-10 minutes prior to washing. For best results, use fresh water and detergent for soak and wash. To Dry: Dryer dry using the Regular Cycle for cotton fabrics and the Permanent Press for synthetic and blended fabrics. Remove promptly from dryer and hang at window. DRAPERIES WITH RUBBERIZED BACKING OR VINYL LAMINATION Follow care instructions on the label. If not available, consider using the soak/wash procedure discussed above. Use only granular laundry detergent, such as Tide. GLASS FIBER CURTAINS To Wash: Soak for 30 minutes in a bath tub or laundry tub using warm (100°F) water and a laundry detergent. Swish gently and rinse well. Also rinse tub thoroughly to remove loose tiny glass fibers. Do not use chlorine bleach. To Dry: Do not wring, dryer dry or iron. Hang curtains over tub to drain excess water. Rehang at window while still damp, gently smoothing hems and seams.

Chart 3.3

ADDITIONAL INFORMATION

Cloths used for cleaning, stain removal, waxing and polishing should be washed separately from other apparel or household items.

Be sure all flammable liquids or solids and their fumes have evaporated prior to washing. Some highly flammable items used in the home include acetone, denatured alcohol, gasoline, kerosene, some liquid household cleaners, spot removers, turpentine, mineral spirits and other items containing volatile solvents.

Do not use a fabric softener on cleaning cloths.

Laundering curtains and washable draperies before they become heavily soiled will help extend their life. Always treat as delicate fabrics, regardless of fiber content, since long exposure to sunlight weakens fibers. Test a small section of the curtain/drapery first and remove braid or trim, if it "bleeds", frays, or puckers during washing.

Dryclean draperies made of acetate, velour, velveteen, damask, silk which may lose their body and luster and/or shrink if laundered.

GLASS FIBER CURTAINS
Curtains and draperies made of glass fibers should not be machine washed and dried. Glass fibers can shed small glass particles which could lodge in fabrics washed in the next load, causing skin irritation.

(Continued)

Special Laundering Instructions *(Continued)*

ITEM	LAUNDERING PROCEDURE
Delicate Fabrics	Follow care instructions on the label. If not available, consider the following: To Wash: Use gentle agitation and spin. If gentle agitation is not available, reduce total wash time. This reduction in mechanical wash action will hurt cleaning. Therefore, increase detergent usage to help compensate for the limited wash action needed to help protect the item. To Dry: Dryer dry using the Delicate Cycle, or hang on a plastic hanger to dry.
Down-Filled Items (Pillows, Jackets, Vests, Sleeping Bags, etc.)	Follow care instructions on the label. If not available, consider the following for washable items: To Wash: Add laundry detergent to the water first and partially fill with warm (100°F) water. Submerge the down-filled item. Balance wash load by adding towels or washing two similarly colored down-filled items (pillows, jackets, vests). Sleeping bags should be washed separately. Complete filling washer. Use regular agitation and normal spin. Stop washer occasionally to press air from the items being washed. To Dry: Dryer dry using low temperature. Add several dry bath towels and a clean pair of tennis shoes to the dryer to help the tumbling action and fluff up the down filling.
Elasticized Apparel (Underwear, Foundation Garments, Support Hose)	Follow care instructions on the label. If not available, consider the following: To Wash: Launder hose separately because of their poor dye stability. Use warm (100°F) water and sufficient amounts of laundry detergent. To Dry: Use lowest heat setting on the dryer and remove while still slightly damp or air dry. Always air dry support hose.

Chart 3.3

ADDITIONAL INFORMATION

Items are considered delicate when they have one or more of the following characteristics:

1. loose fabric construction, such as lace, some knits, etc.
2. unfinished seams
3. loose seam stitching
4. fragilely attached trim

Be consistent in cleaning procedures. Do not alternate drycleaning with water washing. Drycleaning solvents remove the oil from feathers making them brittle. Thus, subsequent agitation during water washing in an automatic washer can break the brittle feathers.

Do not dryclean sleeping bags. Solvent fumes can be a health hazard when using the sleeping bag.

Make certain pillow covers are securely stitched prior to washing.

Clothing worn next to the skin, such as underwear, foundation garments, support hose absorb body oils during wearing. Body oils can damage elastics; therefore, frequent and proper washing is critical to extend the wear life of this clothing.

(Continued)

Special Laundering Instructions *(Continued)*

ITEM	LAUNDERING PROCEDURE
Electric Blankets	Follow Care Label instructions. If not available, consider the following: To Wash: Use gentle agitation and normal spin with warm (100°F) water and a laundry detergent. Help protect the plug by folding and pinning it into a corner of the blanket, thus cushioning the plug from striking the washer basket. To Dry: Most manufacturers of electric blankets recommend air drying by spreading the blankets over two parallel clotheslines or bars.
Heavy Soil *(Work Clothes, Play Clothes, etc.)*	Heavily soiled clothes, regardless of fabric type, require special attention to make them wearable. Items with care instructions advising against the use of hot water and bleach may not be cleaned adequately. To Pretreat: Before washing, ground in soils/stains should be scrubbed with: 1. a liquid laundry detergent, or 2. a paste of granular laundry detergent and water, or 3. a pretreat stain remover, or soaked in warm (100°F) water and a laundry detergent. To Wash: Heavily soiled items should be washed separately from other items with less soil. Use hot (130°F) water, more than the recommended amount of a laundry detergent and the Regular Cycle. Frequently a bleach (chlorine or non-chlorine) is needed to restore the item. To Dry: Dryer dry using the cycle appropriate for the fabric or hang to dry.

Chart 3.3

ADDITIONAL INFORMATION

Avoid drycleaning electric blankets, since solvents can affect the wiring.

(Continued)

Special Laundering Instructions *(Continued)*

ITEM	LAUNDERING PROCEDURE
Hosiery	For washing in an automatic washer, place hosiery in a mesh bag or pillowcase and wash separately from other items to prevent dye transfer. To Wash: Use the Delicate Cycle, warm (100°F) water and a laundry detergent. To Dry: Although usually air dried (support hose should be air dried to help preserve elasticity), hosiery can be dryer dried using low heat. Drying in a mesh bag or pillowcase helps reduce tangling.
Lingerie	Follow instructions on the Care Label. If not available, consider the following: To Wash: Use warm (100°F) water and the Delicate Cycle on the automatic washer. Increase detergent usage to compensate for the reduced water temperature and wash action. To Dry: Dryer dry using low heat or hang to dry.
Mattress Covers/Pads	Follow the care instructions usually provided on the label. If not available consider the following: To Wash: Use regular agitation and spin with warm 100°F water and a laundry detergent. For heavy soils and stains, use a hot (130°F) wash with a chlorine bleach and a laundry detergent. Or soak 30 minutes to overnight in warm (100°F) water using a laundry detergent with enzymes, followed by a fresh warm water wash with a laundry detergent. To Dry: Dryer dry preshrunk mattress pads using the Regular Cycle. Air dry mattress pads made of urethane foam or those having an acetate coating.

Chart 3.3

ADDITIONAL INFORMATION

Hosiery can also be washed by hand using a hand dishwashing detergent. Rinse thoroughly.

Items worn next to the body absorb body oils, thus usually contain more soil than is visible to the eye. The removal of these body oils and odor require wash water temperature of at least 100°F.

White nylon should always be washed only with other white items because it will pick up dye readily from colored items in the wash load.

Use a fabric softener to reduce static cling.

(Continued)

Special Laundering Instructions *(Continued)*

ITEM	LAUNDERING PROCEDURE
Permanent Press	Follow care instructions on the label. If not available, consider the following: To Wash: For normal soil use warm (100°F) water, the recommended amount of a laundry detergent and a cold water rinse. For heavy soil, use more detergent and increase water temperature to hot (130°). Use the Permanent Press Cycle. This cycle automatically cools the thermoplastic fibers prior to the wash spin, provides a cold water rinse and has a shortened or reduced spin speed. These factors are needed to minimize wrinkling. Use a fabric softener to reduce static cling and make apparel more comfortable. To Dry: Dryer dry using the Permanent Press Cycle. Critical to good fabric appearance is the prompt removal of items from the dryer upon cycle completion and immediate hanging/folding.
Pillows	Follow care instructions on label. If not available and pillows are washable, consider the following: To Wash: Partially fill washer with warm (100°F) water and add a laundry detergent. To help maintain a balanced load, submerge two pillows and several bath towels into the wash solution. Completely fill the washer with water and launder using regular agitation and spin. Stop the washer occasionally to press air from the pillows and submerge them in the wash solution. To Dry: Dryer dry "polyester fill" pillows using Regular Cycle. Use low temperature heat when dryer drying down/feather pillows. Air dry foam pillows.

Chart 3.3

ADDITIONAL INFORMATION

Permanent Press is a term used to describe items which resist wrinkling during wear and laundering, but which retain pleats or creases set in by heat during manufacture.

Permanent Press can be made of: 1) 100% synthetic fibers, such as polyester, nylon, acrylic, 2) blends of synthetic fibers and natural fibers, such as cotton, or 3) 100% natural fibers with a resin finish. A resin finish is applied to the natural fiber to give it the wrinkle resistant performance inherent in the synthetic fiber if properly laundered. Some finishes and/or blending of fibers and/or fiber types are more effective than others in minimizing wrinkling.

To minimize wrinkling, do not overcrowd the washer or dryer.

Make certain pillow covers are securely stitched prior to washing.

Kapok pillows should not be laundered since the filling will become lumpy.

(Continued)

Special Laundering Instructions *(Continued)*

ITEM	LAUNDERING PROCEDURE
Plastic *(Shower Curtains, Tablecloths, Furniture Covers, Baby Pants, etc.)*	Follow care instructions on the label. If not available, consider the following: To Wash: Use a granular laundry detergent, such as Tide (anionic surfactants) with warm (100°F) water, regular agitation and spin. A chlorine bleach may be needed for stain removal, such as mildew on outdoor furniture covers, food stains on tablecloths, etc. To Rinse: A warm, instead of cold, water rinse is important to make plastic pliable and more easily handled at the end of the cycle. To Dry: Tumble in the dryer without heat for 5 to 10 minutes with several dry bath towels. Hang to complete drying.
Rubberized or Plastic Coated Fabrics *(Draperies, Sports Apparel, etc.)*	Follow care instructions on label. If not available, consider the following: To Wash: Use a granular laundry detergent, such as Tide (anionic surfactants) with warm (100°F) water, regular agitation and spin. To Dry: Air dry or use limited dryer drying with low heat.
Shoes *(Gym, Aerobic, Jogging)*	Shoes made of rubber, fabric and synthetic materials may be washable in an automatic washer. (Do not launder shoes with leather trim.) Follow Care Label instructions. If not available, consider the following. To Wash: Pretreat spots and stains prior to washing. Launder using warm (100°F) water, granular laundry detergent and regular agitation and spin. Balance load by adding several bath towels. To Dry: Air dry or dry on a stationary rack available with some automatic dryers.

Chart 3.3

ADDITIONAL INFORMATION

Plastic may be affected by sunlight, abrasion, solvents and some detergent surfactants.

These fabric types are coated with rubber or plastic films to reduce air and water penetration and/or improve the insulation properties. These coatings may be affected by sunlight, abrasion, solvents and some detergent surfactants.

(Continued)

Special Laundering Instructions *(Continued)*

ITEM	LAUNDERING PROCEDURE
Table Linens (Tablecloths, Napkins, Placemats, Table Runners, etc.)	Follow care instructions on label. If not available consider the following: To Wash: Use hot (130°F) water for white and colorfast items and warm (100°F) water for non-colorfast items with a laundry detergent. Use the Regular Cycle for sturdy cotton and linen fabrics, the Permanent Press Cycle for synthetic and blended fabrics and the Gentle Cycle for delicates (lace, lace trimmed, embroidered, etc.) To Dry: Tumble dry using the Permanent Press Cycle, if available, or the Regular Cycle, and remove promptly upon cycle completion.
Water Repellent Finishes (All-weather Coats, Sports Apparel, Sleeping Bags, etc.)	Follow care instructions on the label. If not available, consider the following: Pretreat heavily soiled areas as discussed under "Heavy Soil." To Wash: Use warm (100°F) water, the recommended amount of a laundry detergent, the Permanent Press Cycle (regular agitation and slow spin) and a cold rinse. To Dry: Dryer dry using the Permanent Press Cycle or hang on a plastic hanger to dry.

Chart 3.3

ADDITIONAL INFORMATION

Since these items are highly susceptible to food soils and staining, they will need to be exposed to more than normal cleaning procedures to maintain a presentable appearance. Read Care Labels prior to purchase to be certain item can tolerate adequate cleaning procedures (hot water, chlorine bleaching, etc.)

Because of potentially poor dye stability on some of these items, pretreat for stain removal by soaking the entire item and matching accessories in warm (100°F) water using a laundry detergent with enzymes. Avoid rubbing/abrading a small area since this could affect the fabric dye, making it spotty.

Water repellent finishes are applied to fabrics to provide protection from rain or dampness. These finishes may also resist stains.

To Maintain Water Repellent Properties
1. Rinse items thoroughly.
2. Use double the recommended amount of liquid fabric softener.
3. Press thoroughly, using ironing temperature appropriate for the fabric.

Products for Pretreating or Removing Stains Chart 3.4

LAUNDRY PRODUCTS

Laundry Detergents—granules, liquids
Soaps—granules, bars
Bleaches—chlorine: liquids, granules; oxygen: granules, liquids
Presoak Products—granules, liquids
Pretreat Soil and Stain Removers—aerosols, pump sprays, liquids
Detergent Boosters—granules, liquids
Color Removers—granules
For best results, read and follow package instructions carefully

MISCELLANEOUS STAIN REMOVERS

SOLVENTS	OTHERS
Cleaning fluid	Ammonia
Nail polish remover	Baking soda
Denatured alcohol	Rust remover
Rubbing alcohol	White vinegar
Mineral spirits	

SUPPLIES

White paper towels
Clean cloths
Soft bristle brush (toothbrush)
Sponge
Dull knife
Measuring cup and spoons
Medicine/eye dropper

Safe Stain Removal Procedures

—Read instructions on all products and keep them out of children's reach during use and storage. Keep products in original labeled containers. Thoroughly wash any utensil used.

—Do not combine stain removal products, especially ammonia and chlorine bleach; noxious fumes may result.

—Never use a highly flammable solvent, such as gasoline, inside your home; vapors can explode on contact with flames or sparks. Never use chlorinated solvents in or near gas dryers; acid vapors can form, disintegrating fabrics being dried in the dryer.

—Only use solvents, such as cleaning fluid, denatured alcohol or turpentine, in a well-ventilated room, away from open flames and pilot lights. Never inhale these products. Rinse clothes treated with solvents before washing.

Stain Removal Guide for Washable Items

Beverages (Coffee, Tea, Soft Drinks, Wine, Alcoholic)

Sponge or rinse stain promptly in cool water. Pretreat by: 1) soaking with laundry product containing enzymes, or 2) rubbing with a liquid laundry detergent or paste of granular laundry detergent and water. Launder using chlorine bleach, if safe for fabric. Otherwise, soak using an oxygen bleach and the hottest water safe for fabric. Launder.

Blood

Rinse fresh stains in cold running water and rub with bar soap. Rinse again and repeat. For dried stains, first scrape or rub off as much dried blood as possible. Soak remaining blood stains in warm water using a product containing enzymes. Launder. If stain remains, rewash using a bleach safe for fabric.

Candle Wax

Remove surface wax with a dull knife. Place stain between paper towels and press with a warm iron from the back of the fabric. Replace towels frequently to absorb more wax. Then place stain face down on clean paper towels and sponge back of any remaining stain with drycleaning solvent. Let evaporate, then launder. If traces of color remain, wash again using chlorine bleach, if safe for fabric. Otherwise, soak in a solution of oxygen bleach using hottest water safe for fabric, then launder.

Chalk

Brush stain with a moderately soft brush, being careful not to abrade fabric. Wash with a laundry detergent. If stain remains with colored chalk, wash using chlorine bleach, if safe for fabric. Otherwise, soak in a solution of oxygen bleach using the hottest water safe for fabric, then launder.

Chewing Gum, Adhesive Tape, Rubber Cement

Apply ice to harden the stain. When hard, remove as much gum or adhesive as possible by scraping carefully with a dull knife. Place remaining stain face down on paper towels and sponge back of stain with a drycleaning solvent. Rinse, then launder.

Chocolate

Pretreat by soaking or prewashing in warm water using a detergent containing enzymes. If oily stain remains, treat with a liquid laundry detergent or stain remover. Launder. Difficult stains may require using a bleach safe for the fabric.

Chart 3.5

Collar/Cuff Soil

Dampen soil line and rub with bar soap or pretreat with liquid laundry detergent or a paste of granular laundry detergent and water. Launder. If necessary, use bleach safe for fabric.

Cosmetics

Water Based
Dampen stain and rub with bar soap or pretreat with liquid laundry detergent or a paste of granular laundry detergent and water. Launder.

Oil Based
Place stain face down on paper towels. Sponge back of stain with a drycleaning solvent, replacing the paper towel underneath frequently. Dampen stain with water and rub with bar soap. Rinse and launder. If necessary use a bleach safe for the fabric.

Crayon

For a few crayon spots on fabrics, treat the same as candle wax.

For a large load of crayon-spotted clothes, wash with hot water using 1 cup of a laundry soap, such as Ivory Snow, and 1 cup baking soda. If color remains, launder with detergent using a chlorine bleach, if safe for fabric. Otherwise, soak in a solution of oxygen bleach using the hottest water safe for fabric, then launder.

Deodorants and Antiperspirants

Light Stains
Rub in undiluted hand dishwashing liquid detergent, such as Joy. Launder using a low sudsing laundry detergent and the hottest water safe for fabric.

Heavy Stains
Place stain face down on paper towel and alternately sponge back of stain with drycleaning solvent and rub with full strength hand dishwashing liquid, such as Joy. Rinse and repeat until stain is gone. Launder using a low sudsing laundry detergent and hottest water safe for fabric. Use bleach safe for fabric, if necessary.

Special Tips
Avoid staining by: 1) allowing deodorant or antiperspirant to dry on skin before putting on clothes and 2) wearing underarm shields. The build-up of deodorant and antiperspirants can also be reduced by pretreating stained areas on garments with hand dishwashing liquid, such as Joy, every other washing.

(Continued)

Stain Removal Guide for Washable Items *(Continued)*

Dye Transfer

White fabrics stained with dye(s) from a bleeding colored fabric may be restored by using a packaged color remover. Follow the package instructions and do not exceed 160°F water with any synthetic fabrics. If stain remains, launder using a chlorine bleach, if safe for the fabric.

To minimize this type of stain, follow proper sorting and laundering procedures and promptly remove the wash load from the washer at the end of the cycle.

Fabric Softeners

Dampen the stain and rub with bar soap, e.g., Ivory. Rinse. Repeat if necessary and launder.

Fruit Juice

Pretreat by soaking or prewashing in warm water using a detergent containing enzymes. Launder using a bleach safe for the fabric.

Grass

Pretreat by soaking or prewashing in warm water using a detergent containing enzymes. Launder. If stains persist, launder using a bleach safe for the fabric.

Grease, Oil

Pretreat with 1) stain remover, 2) liquid laundry detergent, or 3) paste of granular laundry detergent and water. Launder.

Ink

Determine if ink stain is sensitive to a drycleaning solvent or water by placing a drop of each on the stain. Use the procedure which makes more of the stain flow out of the fabric.

Solvent sensitive inks—ballpoint, felt tip marker, liquid
Pretreat using a prewash stain remover, denatured alcohol or drycleaning solvent. Place stain face down on clean paper towels. Apply stain remover around the back of the stain before applying it directly to the stain. Replace paper towels under stain frequently. Rinse thoroughly. Launder using bleach safe for fabric.

Water sensitive inks—felt tip marker, liquid
Rinse under running cold water to remove as much ink as possible. Rub with bar soap. Wash using laundry detergent, hot water and bleach safe for fabric.

Other inks
Some inks on white fabrics may be removed by using a dye stripper, following package instructions. For stains on colored fabrics, check the fabric dye stability on a hidden area before using dye stripper. Some inks may be impossible to remove.

Chart 3.5

Iodine

Rinse from back of stain with cool water. Soak in solution of color remover if fabric is white (do not use with colored fabrics). Follow package instructions. Rinse and launder.

Mildew

Launder using chlorine bleach, if safe for fabric. If not, soak in an oxygen bleach, then launder.

Mud

When dry, brush off as much as possible. Rinse under cold running water. Pretreat with a paste of granular detergent and water or liquid laundry detergent. Launder using laundry detergent and bleach safe for fabric.

Mustard

Pretreat using a liquid laundry detergent with enzymes, or a spray-type stain remover, or dampen stain with water and rub with bar soap. Rinse and launder using bleach and hottest water safe for fabric.

Nail Polish

Place stain face down on paper towels. Sponge back of stain with nail polish remover, frequently replacing the paper towel under the stain. Repeat the sponging until stain disappears. Launder. (Do not use nail polish remover on acetate or Arnel fabrics. Send them to a drycleaner.)

Paint

Water-based
Rinse fabric in cool water to flush out paint while stains are still wet; then launder. Dried paint cannot be removed.

Oil-based
Pretreat with a solvent recommended on the paint container. If container or label is not available, use mineral spirits. Rinse. Pretreat with a stain remover, bar soap or laundry detergent. Rinse and launder.

(Continued)

Stain Removal Guide for Washable Items *(Continued)*

Perspiration

Pretreat with stain remover or rub with bar soap. If perspiration has changed the color of the fabric, apply ammonia to fresh stains, white vinegar to old stains and rinse. Launder using hottest water safe for fabric. Stubborn stains may respond to washing in a product containing enzymes or oxygen bleach. Treat carefully. Perspiration weakens some fibers such as silk. (Also see stain removal procedures for deodorants and antiperspirants.)

Rust

Do not use chlorine bleach on rust stains or in water containing large amounts of iron.

Few Rust Spots
Apply a rust stain remover available in many supermarkets. Follow manufacturer's instructions. Rinse and launder. Never use rust stain remover containing hydrofluoric acid near or in the washer. It will damage the porcelain enamel finish.

Rust discoloration on entire wash load
Launder using a phosphate detergent and an oxygen bleach.

Severe rust staining
Launder with a commercial rust remover, available at some appliance service companies or commercial cleaning product supply companies. Follow package instructions.

Scorch

Wash using laundry detergent, hot water and chlorine bleach, if safe for fabric. Otherwise, soak in oxygen bleach and hot water, then launder. (Severe scorch is permanent.)

Tar

Scrape residue from fabric with a dull knife. Place stain face down on paper towels. Sponge back of stain with a tar remover or drycleaning solvent. Replace paper towels frequently to absorb more tar and to avoid transferring stains back onto fabric. Launder in hottest water safe for fabric.

Tree Sap

Sponge drycleaning solvent into stain; let dry. Soak stain in a solution of liquid laundry detergent and ammonia. Launder using a liquid laundry detergent.

Tobacco

Dampen stain and rub with bar soap. Pretreat or soak in a product containing enzymes. Launder. If stain remains, launder again using chlorine bleach, if safe for fabric.

Chart 3.5

Typewriter Correction Fluid

Let stain dry thoroughly. Gently brush excess off with a clothes brush. Place stain face down on paper towels and sponge back of stain with thinner designated on the correction fluid bottle. Frequently replace paper towels under the stain. Repeat the sponging until stain disappears. Launder.

Urine, Vomit, Mucus, Feces or Stool

Pretreat or soak in a product containing enzymes. Launder using chlorine bleach, if safe for fabric. Otherwise, use oxygen bleach.

Laundry Products and Aids

PRODUCT CLASSIFICATION	AVAILABLE FORMS*	RECOMMENDED USE
Laundry Products		
SOAPS		
Light Duty	Granular (Ivory Snow)	Designed for lightly soiled items and delicate fabrics. However, light duty soaps are also used for laundering diapers and other baby clothes. Perform best in soft water areas.
Soap Bars	Bars (Ivory)	Pretreating heavy soils and stains prior to laundering. Hand washing lingerie and hosiery are other uses for bar soap.
DETERGENTS		
Heavy Duty	<u>Granular</u> <u>Liquid</u> *Normal Sudsers* (Tide) (Era Plus) (Cheer) (Oxydol) (Dreft) *Medium Sudsers* (Bold 3) (Solo) (Gain) (Liquid Bold 3) *Low Sudsers* (Dash) (Liquid Tide) (Liquid Cheer)	Suitable for all washable fabrics from heavily soiled work clothes to lightly soiled lingerie. Some can be used for hand dishwashing and household cleaning. See specific package instructions. Be sure products containing chlorine bleach and liquid detergents are diluted before using them together. If these products are mixed full-strength, noxious fumes can result.
Light Duty	Granular	Designed for washing delicate fabrics and baby clothes.

*(Procter & Gamble products)

Chart 3.6

GENERAL INFORMATION

Soap for laundering has existed for centuries. Despite improvements made over the years in the quality of the product and in the manufacturing process, all soaps continue to suffer from a major drawback. They combine with water hardness minerals to form a lime soap or soap curd (a sticky white or yellow residue which deposits on the washer and the fabrics in the wash load). This performance negative has led to soap's limited popularity; only a few brands are available today.

A toilet bar (Camay, Zest, Coast, Safeguard) could also be used for pretreating heavy soils and stains and for handwashing lingerie and hosiery.

All heavy duty detergents, regardless of sudsing characteristics, can be used in all top-loading automatic and wringer washers.

Low sudsing detergents were originally designed for tumble-type automatics, where excess suds interfere with the cleaning action of the washer. Now many consumers prefer lower sudsing detergents.

Some liquid laundry detergents (Era Plus, Liquid Tide) provide a convenient form and are especially effective for pretreating oily soils, spots and stains prior to laundering. Other liquid laundry detergents (Bold 3 and Solo) have special ingredients to soften fabrics and reduce static cling.

Granular Tide and the liquids (Bold 3, Era Plus, Cheer, Tide and Solo) contain enzymes to provide additional stain removal benefits. If bleach is used with these products, add the bleach about halfway through the wash for best results.

PERSONAL NOTES

(Continued)

Laundry Products and Aids *(Continued)*

PRODUCT CLASSIFICATION	AVAILABLE FORMS	RECOMMENDED USE
Laundry Aids **BLEACH** Chlorine	Liquid Granular	Can be used on all washable, colorfast, natural fibers (cotton, linen), except protein fibers like wool, silk, mohair and leather. Chlorine bleach is also safe on all washable, colorfast synthetic and permanent press fabrics, except spandex. Chlorine bleach is safe for many colored washable fabrics. Test colors for bleachability prior to washing. Bleach can be added in various ways: 1) to the wash water before the clothes are added, or 2) diluted with a quart (0.95 L) of water and added about halfway through the wash, or 3) to the washer bleach dispenser, following manufacturers' instructions. Be sure products containing chlorine bleach and liquid detergents are diluted before using them together. If these products are mixed full strength, noxious fumes can result. Avoid mixing products containing chlorine bleach with products containing ammonia or acids. Such mixtures can also produce noxious fumes.

Chart 3.6

GENERAL INFORMATION

Liquid chlorine bleach has innumerable uses in housekeeping. Generally whitens fabrics in the laundry. Also aids in soil removal and acts as a disinfectant on most bacteria and viruses likely to be encountered in the home. Its bleaching and disinfecting properties are particularly needed in the kitchen and bathroom. It is ideal for disinfecting and deodorizing diaper pails and removing mildew odor from surfaces.

Applying undiluted bleach directly to fabrics may result in color removal and/or weakening of the fabric.

To determine if a color is bleach safe, apply one drop of a test solution made from 1 tablespoon (15 ml) of a chlorine bleach in ¼ cup (60 ml) of water to an inconspicuous part of the garment, such as a seam allowance. Be sure the solution penetrates the fabric. Let stand for 1 minute and blot dry with a paper towel. If there is no color change, the article can be safely bleached.

Some fabrics may have a chlorine retentive finish, and can become yellowed when chlorine bleach is used. To remove this yellowing, soak item in a plastic container (not an automatic washer) using a packaged color remover (sodium hydrosulfite) and follow manufacturer's instructions. A solution of photographer's "hypo" (sodium thiosulfate) can also be used.

Some nylon fabrics may be permanently yellowed by chlorine bleach.

Do not use chlorine bleach if iron is present in the water supply in excessive amounts because fabric discoloration could occur.

PERSONAL NOTES

(Continued)

Laundry Products and Aids *(Continued)*

PRODUCT CLASSIFICATION	AVAILABLE FORMS*	RECOMMENDED USE
BLEACH *(Continued)* **Oxygen**	Granular (Biz) Liquid	Oxygen bleach is safe for virtually all colored washable fabrics. Oxygen bleach whitens fabrics and aids in soil removal. Oxygen bleaches being milder than the chlorine bleaches work best in hot water or in a soak. As water temperature decreases, exposure time in a soak should be increased. Do not add chlorine bleach to a wash or soak solution containing oxygen bleach. Chlorine bleach stops the bleaching and stain removal action when used in combination with oxygen bleach.
BLUINGS	Liquid	Designed to counteract the natural yellowing of many fabrics. Should be diluted with water prior to adding to the washer at the start of the wash or in the final rinse.
DETERGENT BOOSTERS	Granular Liquid	Designed to reinforce specific performance characteristics desirable in laundering. They should be used in the wash in addition to the recommended amount of detergent. Liquid boosters can also be used for pretreating stains.
FABRIC SOFTENERS	*Washer Added—Liquid* Rinse-added (Downy) Wash-added *Dryer Added* Sheet-type (Bounce) Packet-type	*Rinse-added,* available as triple concentrate (Downy only), regular or dilute liquids, should be added directly to the final rinse. Rinse-added fabric softeners can be added: 1) manually, 2) with an automatic dispenser available on washers or 3) with a reusable plastic ball. Dispensers provide convenience because the fabric softener, although added at the beginning of the cycle, is automatically dispensed into the final rinse. For best performance, fabric softeners do not need water softeners or bluing in the final rinse.

*(Procter & Gamble products)

Chart 3.6

GENERAL INFORMATION

To determine if a color is safe with an oxygen bleach, mix 1 teaspoon (5 ml) oxygen bleach to 1 cup (240 ml) hot water or follow specific instructions on the package. Then place a few drops of test solution on an inconspicuous portion of fabric for 10 minutes. If color does not bleed or there is no color change, oxygen bleach may be used.

Oxygen bleaches usually contain other cleaning ingredients, like water softener (phosphate), enzymes and fabric whitening agents.

Bluing is available as a separate product. Some detergents, such as Cheer, Liquid Cheer, Era Plus, Liquid Bold 3 and Solo also contain a bluing in their formulations.

Fabric softeners impart softness and/or fluffiness to washable fabrics. They also make fabrics feel smooth, decrease static cling, impart a pleasing fragrance, reduce wrinkling and make ironing easier. Used as directed, they are safe for all washable fabrics.

Avoid pouring liquid fabric softener directly on fabrics as staining may occur. If using a dispenser, always dilute with fresh water. With dryer added softeners, stains may result on fabrics if high heat settings are used, especially on small loads of synthetic fabrics. To remove any stain caused by a fabric softener, simply wet and rub stain with bar soap, e.g. Ivory, and launder.

PERSONAL NOTES

(Continued)

Laundry Products and Aids *(Continued)*

PRODUCT CLASSIFICATION	AVAILABLE FORMS*	RECOMMENDED USE
FABRIC SOFTENERS *(Continued)*		*Wash-added* products are designed to be used in the wash portion of the cycle along with detergent or soap. To help prevent potential fabric staining, they should be added to the wash water before the detergent or soap and clothes. These fabric softeners also may be used in the final rinse. *Dryer-added* fabric softeners are designed to be added to a load of clothes in the dryer. With the sheet-type, the heat and tumbling action of the dryer helps to transfer the softener to the clothes. With the packet-type, which is attached to a fin of the dryer drum, the ingredients melt and flow out of the packet, transferring to the clothes during the tumbling action.
PRESOAKS	Granular (Biz)	These products are used for soaking the laundry prior to washing. Since they usually contain enzymes and/or oxygen bleach, they are effective in removing stains and soils. The enzymes are particularly effective in removing proteinaceous stains, such as egg, blood, grass, etc.
PRETREAT SOIL AND STAIN REMOVERS	Aerosol Pump spray Liquid	Designed to pretreat heavily soiled and stained areas.
STARCHES, FABRIC FINISHES AND SIZING	Dry Liquid Spray	The dry and liquid types require mixing with either hot or cold water. They can be used in the washer for large starching jobs or used in a basin for a few articles. The spray types are convenient for use when ironing or for quick touch-up pressing on collars, cuffs and trims.

*(Procter & Gamble products)

Chart 3.6

GENERAL INFORMATION

Some fabric softeners (Bounce) have an unscented version for those who want fragrance-free fabrics.

Presoaks can also be used as a booster in the wash in addition to the recommended amount of detergent.

These products penetrate the fibers and help break up/dissolve grease and oil stains, while the detergent in the subsequent wash helps to disperse the grease mixture and complete the cleaning. Avoid spraying washer/dryer control panels with the petroleum solvent-based pretreaters, since they may cause damage.

These products add a finishing touch to the laundering process. They supply body to fabrics, enhance soil resistance, facilitate soil removal in the next wash and make ironing easier.

Fabric finishes and sizings are formulated especially for synthetic fabrics, since they can be used with lower ironing temperatures suggested for these fabrics.

PERSONAL NOTES

(Continued)

Laundry Products and Aids *(Continued)*

PRODUCT CLASSIFICATION	AVAILABLE FORMS	RECOMMENDED USE
WATER SOFTENERS	Packaged—Granular Mechanical	Designed to be used in the wash with detergents when the water is very hard (over 10.6 grains/gallon). For hard water (7.1 to 10.5 grains/gallon), increasing the amount of recommended detergent is an effective way to tie up water hardness minerals. When soaps are used in hard water, a water softener should be added to both the wash and rinse to help prevent soap curd deposits on fabrics.

Chart 3.6

GENERAL INFORMATION

Water containing relatively large amounts of "hardness" minerals, calcium and magnesium, is known as hard water. Water hardness is expressed either as grains per gallon (gpg) or parts per million (ppm), (1 gpg = 17.1 ppm). This chart classifies the ranges of water hardness:

	Soft	Moderately Hard	Hard	Very Hard
Grains per gallon	0.0–3.5	3.6–7.0	7.1–10.5	10.6+
Parts per million or milligrams per liter	0.0–60	61–120	121–180	181+

Packaged water softener is available in two types: non-precipitating and precipitating.

The non-precipitating type softens water by sequestering hardness minerals and holding them in solution. No visible solid particles form and the water remains clear.

The precipitating type, such as washing soda, softens water by combining with hardness minerals to form a visible, insoluble solid, thus the water looks cloudy. This precipitate can cling to fabrics or washer parts leaving a visible chalky deposit. The precipitating type of water softener should not be used with non-phosphate detergents, since it would increase the likelihood of deposit problems.

Mechanical water softeners, installed in the home, are a practical and effective solution for handling very hard water.

The local water company or County Extension Office can supply information about water hardness in your area.

PERSONAL NOTES

Laundering Problems... Causes, Solutions, Preventive Measures*

PROBLEM	CAUSES
Overall grayness	Insufficient amount of detergent.
	Wash water temperature too low.
	Incorrect sorting— Transfer of soil.
	Transfer of color.
Yellowing— *Build-up of body soil*	Insufficient amount of detergent.
	Wash water temperature too low.
	Treating synthetic fabrics as "delicate" giving them short, gentle, cool washes.
	Handwashing synthetic fabrics with a light duty detergent.

*Developed by The Consumer Affairs Committee of The Soap and Detergent Association

Chart 3.7

SOLUTIONS	PREVENTIVE MEASURES
Increase the amount of detergent and/or use a detergent booster or bleach.	Use a sufficient amount of detergent.
Increase wash water temperature.	Wash in hottest water safe for fabric.
Rewash with an increased amount of detergent and hottest water safe for fabric. Use bleach that is safe for fabric.	Separate heavily soiled items from lightly soiled ones. Use a sufficient amount of detergent, hottest water and bleach safe for fabric.
Do not dry items. Quickly rewash with detergent and a bleach safe for fabric. Severe damage may be permanent.	Sort carefully by color. Separate white or white background prints that are colorfast, colored pastels in solids and prints, medium and bright colors and dark colors.
Increase the amount of detergent and/or use a product containing enzymes, detergent booster or bleach.	Use sufficient amount of detergent.
Increase wash water temperature.	Wash in hottest water safe for fabric.
Wash in hot water, at least 130° F (54° C) using a Permanent Press Cycle (with a cool-down that lowers the water temperature before the first spin). Increase the amount of detergent and/or use a detergent booster or bleach.	Launder frequently and in a washer with water at least 100° F (38° C) with a laundry detergent.
For extremely discolored synthetics that cannot be bleached with chlorine bleach, soak in a product containing enzymes or a detergent booster. Or treat with a color remover by soaking according to package directions. Then wash in washer.	

(Continued)

Laundering Problems... Causes, Solutions, Preventive Measures *(Continued)*

PROBLEM	CAUSES
Fabric discoloration	Use of chlorine bleach on silk, wool or spandex items.
Yellow or brown stains (rust)	Iron and manganese in the water supply.
	Iron in water pipes or water heater.
Blue stains	Failure of a blue coloring in detergent, laundry aid or fabric softener to dissolve or disperse.
Poor soil removal	Insufficient amount of detergent.
	Wash water temperature too low.
	Overloading of washer.
Greasy, oily stains	Insufficient amount of detergent to hold the soil in solution until the end of the wash cycle.
	Wash water temperature too low.
	Fabric softener— Undiluted liquid.

Chart 3.7

SOLUTIONS	PREVENTIVE MEASURES
Yellowing cannot be removed.	Do not use chlorine bleach on silk, wool or spandex items.
To restore discolored load of white clothes, use a rust remover recommended for fabrics. Follow package directions. Repeat if necessary.	Do not use chlorine bleach to remove rust stains. It may intensify discoloration. Use a nonprecipitating water softener in both the wash and rinse water to keep the iron in solution. For an on-going problem, install an iron filter in the water supply system.
Same as above.	Before washing, run the hot water for a few minutes to clear the line. Drain the water heater occasionally.
If caused by a detergent or granular laundry aid, add 1 cup (240 ml) white vinegar to 1 quart (0.95L) of water. Use a plastic container. Soak item for 1 hour; rinse. If caused by fabric softener, rub stains with bar soap; wash.	Add product first, then clothes and start washer. Dilute fabric softener before adding to wash or rinse cycle, or to dispenser.
Increase amount of detergent.	Use a sufficient amount of detergent.
Increase wash water temperature.	Wash in hottest water safe for fabric.
Wash fewer items in a load.	Wash fewer items in a load. Sort clothes by color, fabric and amount of soil. Use proper water level for size of load.
Treat with pretreat stain remover or a liquid laundry detergent. Increase amount of detergent.	Use a sufficient amount of detergent.
Increase wash water temperature.	Wash in hottest water safe for fabric.
Rub fabric softener stains with bar soap; wash.	Don't pour fabric softener directly on fabrics. Dilute rinse cycle fabric softener before adding to the final rinse.

(Continued)

Laundering Problems... Causes, Solutions, Preventive Measures *(Continued)*

PROBLEM	CAUSES

Greasy, oily stains (Continued)	Fabric Softener (Continued)
	  Dryer-added type—
	    Too small a load.
	
	    Improper dryer cycle selection.
	
	    Dryer too hot.

Residue or streaks of powder particularly noticeable on dark or bright colors	Undissolved detergent.
	Some nonphosphate granular detergents can combine with water hardness minerals to form a residue.
Stiff, harsh fabrics. Colored fabrics look faded. Increased fabric wear and abrasion.	In hard water, some nonphosphate granular detergents can combine with water hardness minerals to form a residue.
Lint	Improper sorting, mixing items that give off lint—sweaters, bath towels, flannels—with synthetics, corduroys, velours and other napped fabrics.
	Tissues in pockets.
	Overloading of washer or dryer.
	Insufficient amount of detergent.
	Clogged washer lint filter.

Chart 3.7

SOLUTIONS	PREVENTIVE MEASURES
Rub fabric softener stains with bar soap; wash.	Add a few bath towels to the dryer load to provide proper tumbling.
Same as above.	Use appropriate dryer cycle, i.e., Permanent Press Cycle with polyester/cotton blends, etc.
Same as above.	Reduce dryer temperature. Check dryer instruction booklet to be sure dryer is operating properly.
Add detergent to the washer first, then clothes and start washer.	Same as solution.
Add 1 cup (240 ml) of white vinegar to 1 gallon (3.8 L) warm water. Use a plastic container. Soak item and rinse.	Increase water temperature using hottest water safe for fabric. Do not overload the washer.
	Use a liquid laundry detergent or use a nonprecipitating water softener with a nonphosphate granular detergent.
Add 1 cup (240 ml) of white vinegar to 1 gallon (3.8 L) of warm water. Use a plastic container. Soak item and rinse.	Use a liquid laundry detergent or use a nonprecipitating water softener with a nonphosphate granular detergent.
To help remove severe lint deposition, hand pat dried item using masking or transparent tape. Rewash with detergent and use fabric softener in the final rinse. Dryer dry.	Wash items that give off lint in separate loads from synthetic or napped fabrics. Turning lint collectors inside out may help.
	Wash very heavy lint shedders such as blankets, chenille bedspreads or rugs alone.
Remove tissues and wash items.	Check pockets and remove tissues before laundering.
Wash and dry fewer items in a load.	Same as solution.
Use proper water level for size of load.	Same as solution.
Increase amount of detergent to hold lint in solution during the wash time.	Same as solution.
Clean washer lint filter.	Clean filter after each use.

(Continued)

Laundering Problems . . . Causes, Solutions, Preventive Measures *(Continued)*

PROBLEM	CAUSES
Lint (Continued)	Overdrying in a dryer that creates a build-up of static electricity in synthetic fabrics.
	Dryer lint screen is full.
Holes, tears or snags	Incorrect use of chlorine bleach.
	Unfastened zippers, hooks and belt buckles that readily snag synthetic knits.
	Rips, tears and broken threads in seams.
	Overloading the washer.
	Sun degradation.
Color fading/removal	Surplus/unstable dye.
	Water too hot for colored fabrics.
	Improper use of bleach.
	Undiluted bleach applied directly to fabric.

Chart 3.7

SOLUTIONS	PREVENTIVE MEASURES
Rewash and use a fabric softener in the washer or dryer or use a detergent containing fabric softener in the wash.	Use fabric softener in washer or dryer to reduce static attraction of lint to synthetics.
Remove items from the dryer while they are slightly damp.	Same as solution.
Rewash clothes. Dry in dryer with a cleaned lint screen.	Clean lint screen after each use.
Irreversible condition.	Never pour liquid chlorine bleach directly on clothes. Use the bleach dispenser in the washer or dilute with at least four parts of water before adding to the wash water. For powdered bleach, follow package directions.
Irreversible condition.	Fasten zippers, buckles, hooks and eyes, before adding to the washer. Turn synthetic knits inside out to wash.
May be irreversible if rips, tears and seams cannot be mended.	Mend any visible damage before washing, especially open seams that will fray and become difficult to mend.
May be irreversible if holes, tears and snags cannot be mended.	Let wash load circulate freely. Use the proper water level for the amount of clothes being washed.
Irreversible condition.	Check items like curtains before washing by gently pulling the fabric to determine condition. If curtains can be washed, use Gentle Cycle.
Irreversible condition.	Read Care Label on item. It may not be washable. Test item for colorfastness before washing. Wash new items separately the first few times to remove excess dye.
Irreversible condition.	Use cooler water.
Irreversible condition.	Test item for colorfastness before using bleach. See "Laundry Products and Aids" Pages 89 and 91 for test procedures. Use an oxygen bleach.
Irreversible condition.	Do not pour directly on clothes. Follow directions on package for correct use.

(Continued)

Laundering Problems... Causes, Solutions, Preventive Measures *(Continued)*

PROBLEM	CAUSES
Wrinkling of synthetic/ permanent press fabrics	Failure to use correct cycle.
	Overloading of washer and/or dryer.
	Overdrying.
Shrinking	Overdrying.
	Residual shrinkage.
	Agitation of woolen items.
Pilling	Some synthetic and permanent press items have a natural tendency to "pill" (fibers break off the surface, ball up and cling to the surface rather than break off like natural fibers). This is due to abrasion from normal wear and is commonly found on socks, sweaters, collars, cuffs, underarm areas or any other portion subjected to abrasion.

Chart 3.7

SOLUTIONS	PREVENTIVE MEASURES
Use Permanent Press Cycle on washer and dryer if available. If not, use warm wash and a slower or shorter spin speed. Use cold rinse. Remove items promptly from dryer; hang or fold.	Same as solution.
Allow wash load to move freely in washer and/or dryer.	Do not overload washer and/or dryer. Use fabric softener.
Put clothes back in dryer. Set control for 15-20 minutes on Permanent Press or timed cycle. Heat and cool-down period will remove wrinkles.	Remove clothes promptly after tumble drying.
Irreversible condition.	Reduce drying time and remove clothes when there is a trace of moisture in them. Remove knits, especially cotton, while they are still slightly damp. Stretch back into shape and lay flat to finish drying.
Irreversible condition.	Many knits and woven fabrics can shrink when laundered. Allow for this when purchasing. Also check the quality of the item.
Irreversible condition.	Keep agitation in both wash and rinse cycles at a minimum. Use slow agitation or soak method for washing and rinsing. Regular spinning does not contribute to shrinkage and will speed up drying.
Lint may be attracted to the little balls. To remove the lint, use a lint brush or roller with masking or transparent tape.	Pilling is a wear problem which cannot be prevented completely. It is a natural characteristic of some synthetic and permanent press fabrics. Use a fabric softener in the washer or dryer to lubricate the fibers. When ironing, use a spray starch or fabric finish on collars and cuffs.

4 How to Clean Hard Surfaces

One of the best things about cleaning is that we have an enormous amount of knowledge about this most onerous of household tasks. Experts have studied it relentlessly. Their goal has been to give you better and better results for your efforts—cleaner surfaces, surfaces protected from soil damage, with less demand on your time and aching back. Cleaning may never be anyone's favorite indoor sport, but it is far easier now than it used to be.

In organizing your cleaning, approach it this way, in three steps:

1. Know your surfaces.

2. Know your problems.

3. Know the right products.

Cleaning may never be anyone's favorite indoor sport, but it is far easier now than it used to be.

Knowing the surfaces in your home may sound simple and easy, something you grasp at a glance. Maybe so. But maybe not. Modern technology has created remarkable look-alike substitutes—handsome, durable, reasonable in price, easy to clean. Excellent surfaces, but not necessarily what they appear to be.

Kitchen cabinets looking for all the world like wood are metal with wood grain stenciled into the finish. The storm door

107

that traditionally had a glass window now sports a look-alike synthetic that won't shatter. Counter tops are made of—what? In the bathroom, is the marble really marble? Is the kitchen floor rubber, plastic, or something else?

What to do?

The best thing to do, when you have the slightest doubt about a surface, is to go directly to the people who know the facts. Ask the builder of the home. Ask the manufacturer or dealer who sold you an appliance. If you are taking over someone else's home, ask the departing occupant. In an apartment, ask the superintendent.

Different surfaces may require different cleaning products and methods. So getting the facts straight is the logical first step in organizing your cleaning program.

This chapter consists mainly of two lists. Chart 4.1 (Cleaning Hard Surfaces in the Home) Pages 112-127 describes various hard surfaces in the home and how to clean them. (Hard surfaces are floors, counter tops, cabinets, walls—versus soft surfaces such as carpets, upholstered furniture.)

Chart 4.2 (Household Cleaning Products) Pages 128-135 describes products, their recommended use and general information about each one. If used correctly, these products produce little miracles for us. Misused, they turn minor problems into major ones.

These charts are easy to understand and can be invaluable. Two suggestions about using the charts.

First, read both from beginning to end at one sitting. It will take less than an hour. This will give you a chance to see the differences between surfaces, problems and products, and thus see how they relate to your home. If you read the lists bit by bit, setting them aside and then coming back, it is easy to lose track of these important differences.

Second, make notes as you read. When you come to a surface that is in your home, flag it with a circle. When you recognize a situation you contend with, make another circle. Nobody can remember all these bits of information, so the pencil marks will help you find the relevant copy when you refer to the lists later.

4/How to Clean Hard Surfaces

Here is another suggestion. In Chapters 1 and 2, we urged you to make a schedule for the cleaning jobs in your home, describe the nature of these cleaning problems and define the types of products to deal with them. Have those documents handy as you read these new lists, and change them if you find new information here that gives you a more accurate picture.

Now turn to the lists on Pages 112-135.

Little Tips About Cleaning

It is easier to clean soil when it is fresh than after it has hardened.

- *Clean regularly and often.* It is easier to clean soil when it is fresh than after it has hardened. And, the longer soil is left to harden, the more likely it will be ground into the surface and cause real damage (to floors, for example). Another reason is probably the most important: Frequent cleaning becomes habit, second nature, the accepted routine. If you can organize yourself into a good habit, half the battle is won.

- *Remove loose soil.* Before you clean a floor, sweep up or vacuum dust and crumbs. It will make cleaning less messy, and you'll get better results.

- *When cleaning floors:*

  — plan your strategy to end up by an exit door (not stranded in a corner waiting for the floor to dry);

  — clean a small area of the floor (about 3 feet square) at a time, using firm strokes;

  — allow the clean surface to dry thoroughly, then apply wax or polish if the flooring requires.

- *Soak soiled items.* A barbeque grill or oven rack tends to get coated with burnt-on food. Soak it several hours in a solution of all-purpose cleaner and water. It will loosen the soil.

- *Don't let cleaning solution stand too long.* Allow the cleaning solution to stay on the surface just long enough to loosen soil, then wipe it off. Leave it on too long and it might damage the surface.

- *Beware of scratching.* Heavy scrubbing or scouring can cause scratches on painted, laminated and tile surfaces. Usually, an easy motion is enough.

- *Change the solution when necessary.* In cleaning, the dirt you remove becomes suspended in the cleaning solution. If the water gets too dirty, some of the dirt will get redeposited as smudges, streaks or film. So make sure the solution and cloth/applicator you are using to clean are also clean.

- *Rinse as necessary.* Follow the package directions. As a rule, rinsing is not necessary if the cleaning product is diluted with water. When used full-strength, or if the surface is heavily soiled, rinsing helps prevent streaking or filming.

- *Get an extra shine.* An all-purpose household cleaner and water will effectively clean ceramic tile, laminated surfaces, porcelain and high-gloss painted surfaces. If you want an extra shine, buff dry with paper towels or a soft cloth.

Chapter 4

Related Charts

Chart 4.1   Cleaning Hard Surfaces in the Home
Chart 4.2   Household Cleaning Products

Cleaning Hard Surfaces in the Home

SURFACE	END USE	CLEANING PROCEDURE
Asphalt	Flooring	Asphalt is a resilient flooring. To clean, wipe floor surface with a slightly damp mop, rag or sponge which has been wrung out in the recommended amounts of an all-purpose household cleaning solution. Follow package instructions for extra dirty floors where more household cleaning detergent is needed. Change detergent solution as necessary if the floor is very dirty. Minimum amounts of water should be used. Excess water may penetrate between the seams of sheet-type flooring or between individual tiles causing a loosening of the adhesive and, eventually, warping and cracking of the flooring material. Avoid highly abrasive cleaning products which can scratch the surface forming indentations that can collect future dirt. Generally, rinsing isn't necessary. However, follow specific flooring manufacturer's instructions and package instructions on cleaning products regarding rinsing recommendations.
Ceramic	Bathtubs Sinks Tile (Walls, Floors) Toilet Bowls	*Bathtubs, sinks* Wet the surface to be cleaned. Sprinkle cleanser onto the surface and let stand for a minute or so to allow ingredients to attack the soil and stains. Rub/scour as needed and rinse. If stains remain, repeat procedure. *Ceramic tile in walls and floors* Wipe tiles to remove soapy film, using a household cleaner (either diluted or full strength), spray-type cleaner or vinegar/water solution (4 parts water to 1 part vinegar). Rinse thoroughly with clean water and buff tiles to prevent streaking. Using a small brush, clean grouting with full strength liquid household cleaner, or cleanser. With badly stained or moldy grouting, try a solution of liquid chlorine bleach (¾ cup per gallon water). Apply solution with a cloth or sponge to help prevent splattering on clothes or nearby fabric. Do not combine liquid household cleaner and chlorine bleach.

Chart 4.1

SPECIAL INFORMATION

Asphalt Tile is attractive and low cost. Made of asbestos fibers, resin and/or asphalt, the color extends throughout the tile. These tiles can be installed directly over concrete foundation slabs or basement floors. Greasy oily soils and solvents will attack asphalt and cause softening of the tile and sometimes color bleeding. Therefore paste wax or solvent based liquid wax should not be used. Use special waxes specifically designed for asphalt tile.

PERSONAL NOTES

(Continued)

Cleaning Hard Surfaces in the Home *(Continued)*

SURFACE	END USE	CLEANING PROCEDURE
Ceramic (Continued)		*Toilet Bowls* Sprinkle toilet bowl liberally with cleanser and scour with a toilet brush, making sure to clean up under the inside rim of the bowl. Let stand for a few minutes. Flush using the brush to rinse down the sides of the bowl. To clean the outside of the bowl, sprinkle cleanser on a wet cloth or sponge and rub on lightly. Rinse cloth or sponge and wipe off the surface. All-purpose cleaners may also be used to clean the outside of the bowl.
Concrete	Flooring Outdoor Furniture Walls	Wet surface with clean water first before washing. Then wash with an all-purpose household cleaner following package instructions and rinse thoroughly. Although concrete has the appearance of a hard surface, it is usually porous and should be sealed to prevent various materials from being absorbed into the pores.
Cork	Flooring Wall Coverings	Use a solvent or liquid cleaning wax which contains a solvent and wax. Follow use instructions on these products and the cork manufacturer's instructions.
Glass	Cabinet Doors Mirrors Skylights (flat) Table Top Protectors Thermopane Windows Windows	Wash with a solution of warm water and ammonia (½ cup ammonia with 1 gallon water) using a lint free cloth. Remove wash solution with a squeegee wiping the squeegee with a clean cloth after each stroke. Or use a special glass cleaner following package instructions.
Linoleum	Flooring	Linoleum is a resilient flooring. For suggested cleaning procedure, see ASPHALT. Wax helps protect floor.

Chart 4.1

SPECIAL INFORMATION

PERSONAL NOTES

Avoid acids which can cause pitting or loss of strength of the flooring.

Avoid the use of water.

Avoid abrasives that could scratch or mar the surface.

Linoleum is one of the first man-made flooring materials made, but today is in limited production, if any. The name, however, has become a common, almost generic, term to describe many types of resilient flooring.

(Continued)

Cleaning Hard Surfaces in the Home *(Continued)*

SURFACE	END USE	CLEANING PROCEDURE
Metals—Common		
Aluminum	Appliance Trim Drip Pans Ranges Reflector Bowls	*For all common metals* Wash with a solution of detergent or all-purpose cleaner, or use a metal cleaner specifically designed for the metal being cleaned. Follow package instructions. Rinse with a cloth wrung from clear water and dry with a soft cloth.
Chrome Plated Steel	Appliance Trim Oven & Grill Racks Small Portable Appliances	
Painted Steel	Cabinets Exterior of Appliances (Dishwashers, Dryers, Ranges, Refrigerators, Washers) Interior of Dryers Small Portable Appliances	
Stainless Steel	Appliance Trim Dishwasher Interiors Drip Pans Range Tops Reflector Bowls Sinks	
Metals—Special		
Brass and Copper	Bowls Buckets Candlesticks Cookware (copper) Decorative objects Trivets	Wash in hot sudsy water using a laundry detergent or hand dishwashing liquid. Rinse with hot water and dry immediately using a soft cloth. For the removal of heat discoloration or tarnish, use a specially designed copper cleaner and follow package instructions. Use on unlacquered metals only.

Chart 4.1

SPECIAL INFORMATION

For aluminum and chrome plated steel
For heavily soiled surfaces, such as reflector bowls or drip pans on ranges and oven racks, soak and wash in a hot detergent solution, rinse and dry.

Burned on food soils on the metal ring around electric surface units can be removed by scouring with a cleanser or rubbing with a scouring pad. Soaking with a concentrated solution of automatic dishwashing detergent will help soften the burned on food.

For chrome plated steel only
Adding ammonia to the detergent solution will help loosen heavy soils. Do not use ammonia on aluminum.

Stainless Steel dishwasher interiors
Some dishwasher models have stainless steel interiors; others are porcelain or plastic. Regardless of finish, these surfaces are automatically cleaned with specifically formulated dishwasher detergent each time the dishwasher is run. If special cleaning is necessary, use only detergents specifically designed for automatic dishwashers.

Avoid scratching brass or copper surfaces. Use a soft bristled brush (toothbrush). Do not use steel wool or other abrasives.

Often brass or copper decorative items have a lacquered finish. Use special cleaners only on unlacquered metals.

PERSONAL NOTES

(Continued)

Cleaning Hard Surfaces in the Home *(Continued)*

SURFACE	END USE	CLEANING PROCEDURE
Painted	Baseboards Dry Walls Molding Wood Door Frames	Wash an inconspicuous area to determine washability of the surface. Use a solution of all-purpose cleaner, following package instructions. Apply only enough pressure to remove soil. Wash from the bottom up to prevent streaking from the dirty cleaning solution running down the wall. These streaks may be impossible to remove. Finger prints and tough spots may require full strength liquid or spray cleaners. Rinse well.
Plastic	Decorative Accessories Furniture Window Sills	Wipe the surface with a cloth or sponge wrung from a solution of detergent or all-purpose cleaner, following package instructions. A moderately soft brush will help in cleaning webbing or any textured plastic surface.
	Appliance Interiors (Refrigerator, dishwasher, oven, microwave) Appliance Trim Portable Appliances Washers	*Refrigerator/freezer interiors* Turn off/unplug appliance. Remove food and shelves/baskets, etc. Wash interior walls, racks, drawers, door shelves, baskets, etc., with a solution of 1 tablespoon baking soda to 1 quart of warm water. (Odor free detergents are recommended to prevent off odors from developing in stored foods. Baking soda will also leave surfaces free of odor.) Rinse these surfaces with clear water and wipe dry. Prior to washing the freezer interior, non-defrosting models will need to be defrosted when frost build-up is about ½ inch thick. Defrosting can be speeded up by placing pans of hot water in the freezer. Refill pans as water cools. Allow frost to melt off. Never chip off frost and risk puncturing the freezer lining. Do not speed up defrosting by using portable heat sources, such as fans, hair dryers. Melting water dripping near electrical appliances creates a safety hazard. *Plastic dishwasher interiors* Some dishwasher models have plastic interiors, others are stainless steel or porcelain. Regardless of finish, these surfaces (Continued next page)

Chart 4.1

SPECIAL INFORMATION

Test washability first. Some paint becomes less washable with age.

Avoid scratching plastics and plastic laminates with an abrasive cleanser

Avoid using stain removal sprays containing solvents near laundry appliances with plastic control panels. Solvents can damage these surfaces.

PERSONAL NOTES

(Continued)

Cleaning Hard Surfaces in the Home *(Continued)*

SURFACE	END USE	CLEANING PROCEDURE
Plastic (Continued)		are automatically cleaned with specifically formulated dishwashing detergent each time the dishwasher is run. If special cleaning is necessary, use only detergents specifically designed for automatic dishwashers. *Ovens* *Continuous Cleaning*—Follow the range manufacturer's specific instructions. Generally they can be wiped with a wet sudsy (hand dishwashing liquid or all-purpose cleaner solution) sponge; rinse thoroughly and blot dry. *Microwave*—Follow the range manufacturer's instructions. Generally they can be cleaned by wiping with a wet sudsy (hand dishwashing liquid or all-purpose cleaner) cloth/sponge. Rinse.
	Bathtubs Faucets Shower Stalls Sinks Spas Wall Tile	*Bathtubs/Shower Stalls, Faucets, Whirlpool Bathtubs and Spas* To clean hard-to-remove soap scum, use liquid all-purpose cleaners full strength or a granular all-purpose cleaner diluted (¼ cup/gallon of water). Then rinse. *Fiberglass Bathtubs/Shower Stalls* To clean, use only mild abrasive powder or liquid cleansers. Sprinkle or squeeze cleanser onto surface or damp sponge. Rub surface gently. Rinse or wipe clean. For extra tough soils, let product set on surface for 30 seconds to allow product to loosen dirt.
	Clocks Skylights (domed) Windows/Storm Doors	*Some transparent plastic used for windows/storm doors, domed skylights and face covers of clocks* Use a cleaning product designed especially for this material or wash using a solution of hand dishwashing detergent.
	Plastic Laminates Cabinets Counter Tops Furniture	Wipe the surface with a cloth or sponge wrung from a solution of detergent or all-purpose cleaner, following package instructions.

Chart 4.1

SPECIAL INFORMATION

PERSONAL NOTES

Comet and Mr. Clean Cleanser have been specially formulated with milder, safer-to-use abrasives and are recommended by Owens-Corning for regular cleaning on their Fiberglas® bathing fixtures and by Elkay for use on their stainless steel sinks.

Avoid using laundry detergents, household cleaners, cleansers and ammonia to clean plastic windows/storm doors. The alkalinity of these products could cause permanent opaque streaking in the plastic.

Plastic laminate counters and table tops are heat sensitive so can be damaged by a hot iron or pan.

(Continued)

Cleaning Hard Surfaces in the Home *(Continued)*

SURFACE	END USE	CLEANING PROCEDURE
Porcelain	Bathtubs Exterior Surfaces of Appliances Interior of Dishwashers Ovens Oven and Grill Racks Range Tops Sinks	*Bathtubs, sinks* Apply liquid cleansers directly to the surface to be cleaned. With granular cleanser, wet the surface first, then apply cleanser on the surface and let stand for a minute or so to allow ingredients to attack the soil and stains. Rub/scour as needed and rinse. If stains remain, repeat procedure. *Range tops, ovens, oven and grill racks* Range cleaning can be made easier by wiping up spills/splatters after each use. Wipe range top and cooled oven using an all-purpose or light duty liquid detergent solution. Rinse and dry. For heavily soiled ovens, designed to be manually cleaned, scour with a cleanser or use a specially formulated product designed for cleaning ovens. (For continuous cleaning ovens, follow range manufacturer's instructions. Also see ovens in plastic section. Follow range manufacturer's instructions for self-cleaning ovens). Soaking oven and grill racks in a detergent solution plus household ammonia will help loosen these usually more heavily soiled surfaces. Follow with spot cleaning using a liquid or granular cleanser. *Exterior surfaces of refrigerator, freezer, washer, dryer, dishwasher* Wipe regularly with a solution of a detergent or all-purpose cleaner to prevent a build-up of soil requiring harsher cleaning methods. Rinse, if desired, and polish with a dry cloth. *Porcelain dishwasher interiors* Some dishwasher models have porcelain interiors; others are plastic or stainless steel. Regardless of finish, these surfaces are automatically cleaned with specifically formulated dishwasher detergents each time the dishwasher is run. If special cleaning is necessary, use only detergents specifically designed for automatic dishwashers.

Chart 4.1

SPECIAL INFORMATION

Acid-based products may be useful to help remove rust and other built-up water hardness mineral stains. Do not mix these products with products containing chlorine bleach.

Wax occasionally with an appropriate wax (refer to manufacturer's recommendations). Waxing will: 1) help repel soil, 2) protect the finish and 3) make future cleaning easier.

PERSONAL NOTES

(Continued)

Cleaning Hard Surfaces in the Home *(Continued)*

SURFACE	END USE	CLEANING PROCEDURE
Rubber	Flooring	Rubber is a resilient flooring. For suggested cleaning procedures see ASPHALT.

Stone
  Marble
  Terrazzo
	Flooring
	Window Sills
		Wet surfaces with clean water first before washing. Then wash with an all-purpose cleaner following package instructions and rinse thoroughly. With improper rinsing, crystals can form in the pores of the surface after drying. These crystals may then exert pressure and cause a spalling or chipping of the surface.

Vinyl	Flooring	Vinyl is a resilient flooring. For suggested cleaning procedure, see ASPHALT. *Vinyl—No Wax* Solvent-based waxes and polishes, including paste wax, should not be used on vinyl floors. Some flooring manufacturers recommend applying vinyl dressings or finishes to restore shine to heavy traffic areas. *Vinyl, waxable and Vinyl asbestos* Needs a regular application of a floor polish to help protect the floor surface. Do not use solvent-based waxes and polishes including paste wax.

Chart 4.1

SPECIAL INFORMATION

Rubber Tile is expensive and not widely used. Generally made of synthetic rubber, resins, pigments and curing agents, rubber tile has a natural resilience that cushions footsteps and absorbs sound. While rubber tile deteriorates on exposure to strong sunlight, waxing will help minimize the problem. As with asphalt tile, greasy oily soils and solvents will soften the rubber tile and possibly cause color bleeding. Paste wax or solvent based liquid wax should not be used on rubber tile. Use special waxes specifically designed for these tiles.

Avoid acids which can cause pitting.

Vinyl Flooring is the most widely used flooring today and is available with and without minimum care finishes.

Conventional Vinyl Flooring is available in a wide range of colors, patterns, construction quality and price. Thin vinyl with only surface depth color is less expensive than thicker vinyl where color extends throughout the thickness. Thicker vinyl wears better, but is more expensive. Cushioned backing is available with vinyl and helps provide a quieter and more comfortable surface.

Minimum Care Vinyl (commonly called No-Wax) is the most popular type of flooring used today. It has a clear protective coating (often dimpled or embossed) on the surface to help reduce abrasion, thus preserving the color and pattern of conventional vinyl. The coating reflects light which is the basis of the shine. Various shine levels ranging from high gloss to no shine at all are available. Wax should never be used on this type of flooring.

PERSONAL NOTES

(Continued)

Cleaning Hard Surfaces in the Home *(Continued)*

SURFACE	END USE	CLEANING PROCEDURE
Wallpaper	Wall Covering	*Washable Wallpaper* Use a special liquid wallpaper cleaner following package instructions. Work from the bottom up to prevent streaking from the dirty cleaning solution running down the wall. These streaks may be impossible to remove. *Non-washable wallpaper* Do not wash. There are dry pads (art gum ground up in a mesh bag) available for cleaning non-washable wallpaper. Or use a dough-like wallpaper cleaner, available in some hardware stores. Follow package instructions.
Wood	Cabinets Flooring Furniture Wall Covering Window Blinds	*Flooring, wallpaneling* Use a solvent or liquid cleaning wax which contains a solvent and wax. Follow use instructions on these products. *Furniture* Dust frequently. Use specially formulated products following package recommendations. The use of polish or wax depends on the finish of the wood. For natural oil finishes rub with boiled linseed, lemon or tung oil. Avoid waxing natural oil finishes.

Chart 4.1

SPECIAL INFORMATION

Wash an inconspicuous area to determine washability of the surface.

Avoid the use of water or abrasives, since these will damage wood.

PERSONAL NOTES

Household Cleaning Products

PRODUCT CLASSIFICATION	AVAILABLE FORMS*	RECOMMENDED USE
All-Purpose Cleaners	Granular (Spic and Span) Liquid (Mr. Clean) (Spic and Span Pine) (Top Job) Spray	Granules or liquids, when mixed with water are designed to clean fairly large washable surfaces, such as floors, countertops, painted walls, etc., where accumulations of soil are relatively uniform. For heavy soiling, more concentrated solutions can be prepared. Liquids may also be used full strength. Granules can also be sprinkled onto a damp sponge or cloth, or on the surface to be cleaned, to remove stubborn dirt without scratching. Sprays in aerosol or in pump-actuated bottles are convenient to clean smaller areas.
Carpet Cleaners	Aerosol Spray Liquid	Designed to wet the pile of the rug and take up oily and greasy soils. They provide a dense foam that traps soil in suspension and dries to a brittle solid residue which can be removed by a vacuum cleaner.
Carpet Fresheners	Aerosol Spray Granular	These products are not intended to provide cleaning but are designed to counteract malodors residing in carpets. The product is spread over the carpet, allowed to dry for a few minutes and then vacuumed. Follow manufacturer's instructions.
Cleansers	Granular (Comet) Liquid (Mr. Clean Cleanser)	Designed to remove relatively heavy soil accumulations often found in small areas. (Pots and pans, stove tops with baked-on food residue, sinks, toilets, porcelain or fiberglass bathtubs, showers, etc.) Contains fine abrasive ingredients to provide effective scouring action.

*(Procter & Gamble products)

Chart 4.2

GENERAL INFORMATION

Some products in this category have disinfecting and deodorizing benefits (Spic and Span Pine).

For general cleaning, sprays, granules and liquids when diluted with water, require no rinsing. If used full strength, rinsing is recommended. Follow manufacturer's instructions.

Available in concentrated or ready-to-use liquids and aerosol sprays. Follow manufacturer's instructions.

The principal ingredient in carpet fresheners is a pleasing fragrance and in the case of granules it is on a carrier, such as borax or baking soda.

Since cleansers contain a fine abrasive, they are suited to many demanding cleaning jobs. However, they can mar very delicate surfaces. Avoid the use of cleansers on sterling silver or silverplate, china, mirrors and glass, non-stick finishes on cookware, acrylic and plastic coated surfaces.

Comet and Mr. Clean Cleanser have been specially formulated with milder, safer-to-use abrasives and are recommended by Owens-Corning for regular cleaning on their Fiberglas® bathing fixtures and by Elkay for use on their stainless steel sinks.

PERSONAL NOTES

(Continued)

Household Cleaning Products *(Continued)*

PRODUCT CLASSIFICATION	AVAILABLE FORMS*	RECOMMENDED USE
Disinfectants	Liquid (Spic and Span Pine)	These products contain germicides, usually selected from the group including pine oil, phenolics and coal tar derivatives. Designed to clean and deodorize hard surfaces in the home when diluted with water. Used full strength they offer disinfecting performance. Follow manufacturer's package instructions.
Drain Cleaners	Granular Liquid	Chemically strong products designed to unclog kitchen drains which are obstructed with grease and other types of materials, preventing the free flow of water. Follow manufacturer's instructions precisely and keep package closed between uses.
Glass Cleaners	Liquid Spray	Follow manufacturer's instructions for use on mirrors and windows. For streak-free surfaces, wipe dry with a non-linting fabric or paper towels. Some of these products can cause a permanent opaque hazing on plastic surfaces (windows, storm doors, clock face protectors, etc.)
Insecticides	Crystal Hanging device Spray	Follow manufacturer's instructions.
Metal Cleaners	Liquid Paste Spray	Special cleaners for different metals are available. Follow package instructions carefully.
Oven Cleaners	Liquid Sponge Spray	Designed to help remove charred grease and other food components deposited on oven walls. In most oven cleaners designed to work in cold ovens, soil removal requires strong chemicals. Other types, with less strong chemicals, require oven heat to effect soil removal. Regardless of the type, follow package instructions precisely.

*(Procter & Gamble products)

Chart 4.2

GENERAL INFORMATION

Used in the laundry for extra cleaning and deodorizing performance, these products should be added to the washload along with the laundry detergent.

Packaged in containers with trigger pump sprays to provide easy dispensing.

Moth and insect control depend upon cleanliness and good moth and insect repellant products.

A mild abrasive is present in some metal cleaners to aid in the mechanical removal of tarnish and soil and to act as a polishing/buffing agent. Some products also contain an antioxidant which protects the cleaned metalware against rapid re-tarnishing.

Packaged in aerosol containers, pump-actuated bottles or squeeze-actuated sponge, these products are formulated to be as thick as possible to promote clinging to vertical oven surfaces.

PERSONAL NOTES

(Continued)

Household Cleaning Products *(Continued)*

PRODUCT CLASSIFICATION	AVAILABLE FORMS	RECOMMENDED USE
Toilet Bowl Cleaners	Crystal In-tank cleaner Liquid	Designed to help maintain a clean and pleasant smelling toilet bowl. Some products also disinfect. Follow package instructions for use and disposal precisely.

Traditional Cleaners	Liquid
	  Ammonia
	  Bleach
	  Vinegar
	
	Granular
	  Baking Soda
		For both general and specific cleaning tasks, these traditional cleaning aids should be used separately with water and not mixed with other chemicals or formulated products.
		
		Ammonia, a weak volatile alkali, leaves no solid residue on drying, provides good window (glass) cleaning characteristics.
		
		Baking Soda, a weak alkali, aids in the removal of burned on soils on cookware. It also absorbs odors arising from foodstuffs stored in the refrigerator.
		
		Bleach is the only exception to mixing with other products. Chlorine bleach, when used along with laundry detergents, is effective in removing stains on fabrics. Bleach is also effective on stains, especially mildew, found on hard surfaces in the home.
		
		Vinegar, a mild acid, is often effective on hard water deposits.

Chart 4.2

GENERAL INFORMATION

Toilet bowl cleaners have experienced a great expansion in recent years. As a result there are many different product forms. The thickened liquids cling to the sides of the toilet bowl to aid in soil removal with a brush. Bowl fresheners help to keep the bowl smelling fresh. In-tank cleaners dispense ingredients to the toilet bowl with each flush of the toilet.

Regardless of the many new product types available, toilet bowls may still require an occasional scouring with a cleanser, such as Comet.

NEVER COMBINE A TOILET BOWL CLEANER WITH A CHLORINE BLEACH. TOXIC FUMES RESULT AND MAY CAUSE ILLNESS.

Specifically formulated products, such as Mr. Clean, Spic and Span and Top Job, will clean better than ammonia or vinegar. In fully formulated products, manufacturers also have the opportunity to provide multiple benefits with advantages in performance and convenience. Ammonia, vinegar and chlorine bleach have characteristic strong odors which may be more objectionable than odors from formulated products.

Avoid mixing chlorine bleach with products containing ammonia or acids. Such mixtures can produce noxious fumes. Be sure products containing chlorine bleach and liquid detergents are diluted before using them together. If these products are mixed full strength, noxious fumes can also result. Do not combine chlorine bleach with toilet bowl cleaners. Do not mix vinegar with ammonia or chlorine bleach.

PERSONAL NOTES

(Continued)

Household Cleaning Products *(Continued)*

PRODUCT CLASSIFICATION	AVAILABLE FORMS	RECOMMENDED USE
Tub, Tile and Sink Cleaners	Liquid Spray	Speciality products formulated to remove hard water deposits, soap scum, rust stains and discolorations due to mold growth which are most often encountered on bathroom surfaces.
Upholstery Cleaners	Aerosol Spray Granular Liquid	See Carpet Cleaners.
Waxes and polishes	Aerosol Spray Liquid Paste	Designed to protect surfaces and often help delay heavy cleaning. Follow manufacturer's instructions.

Chart 4.2

GENERAL INFORMATION

Available as pump-actuated sprays, liquids and aerosol products. Some sprays are dispensed as foams to reduce fast run-off on vertical surfaces.

There are many different types designed for specific uses. Some are to be used in furniture care, others for floor care, and still others for care of metal finishes. Products are available to clean and others provide a protective top coat. Some products provide both of these benefits.

PERSONAL NOTES

5 How To Plan Better Dishwashing

For a job that is done at least a thousand times a year in most homes, it is not surprising experts have focused so much study on finding the best methods and products to make dishwashing easier, more effective and far less time-consuming. A good thing it is, too. Short on fun and never ending, dishwashing can use all the help it can get. (Incidentally, dishes like floors and walls are other hard surfaces in the home.)

This chapter tells how to wash dishes by hand and with an automatic dishwasher. In both cases, it is essential to organize your work and supplies before you lift a finger. To help get yourself ready, you will find five charts: Chart 5.1 (Dishwashing Products and Aids); Chart 5.2 (Hand Dishwashing Supplies); Chart 5.3 (Hand Dishwashing Problems, Causes and Solutions); Chart 5.4 (Cleaning Dishwashable Items); Chart 5.5 (Dishwasher Problems, Causes, Solutions, Preventive Measures).

Why Wash Dishes?

A good place to start is to get our minds straight on why dishwashing is such an important function in a well-kept home. First, it is a matter of good health—bacteria grow rapidly on

> *Everybody feels just a little bit better in a clean home, and what gives you a better sense of tidiness than having a kitchen where everything is clean and in its place?*

dishes and utensils that have not been properly cleaned, and dirty dishes attract roaches and other pests. Second, as a practical matter, pots and skillets and other cooking equipment conduct heat more evenly and efficiently when they are spotless. Third, items kept clean and in good condition last much longer and save you the cost of replacing them.

A fourth point is this: Everybody feels just a little bit better in a clean home, and what gives you a better sense of tidiness than having a kitchen where everything is clean and in its place?

Organizing for Dishwashing

Now let's get started with a few important dishwashing preliminaries. These apply to both hand and automatic dishwashing.

1. Scrape away food particles or excess soil from dishes, pots, pans, skillets.

2. Use a paper towel or rubber spatula to remove as much grease as possible. Put the grease into an old coffee can or other heat-resistant container—but not down the sink drain because that could cause clogs and other plumbing trouble.

3. Soak heavily soiled pans and utensils in a hot water solution of dishwashing liquid detergent or automatic dishwashing detergent for 30 minutes or so.

4. There are two ways of disposing of loosened food particles, and one way *not*. Pour the soaking water through the sink drain to catch the particles, or pour the entire contents into the food waste disposer. But do *not* pour the soak water down the sink drain with no strainer or garbage disposer present as the food particles might settle in crooks of the plumbing and cause trouble.

5. Wash out coffee and tea pots thoroughly after each use to avoid a bitter taste that might otherwise linger. Rinse thoroughly.

5/How to Plan Better Dishwashing

6. Don't forget to wipe the sink and counter tops with a detergent solution. That's where you handle food and dishes, so they must be clean and sanitary. Check the detergent package for instructions to make sure you have the right product for these surfaces.

This is a good time to get acquainted with the products for both hand dishwashing and automatic dishwashing. Chart 5.1 (Dishwashing Products and Aids) Pages 144-147 is well worth reading all the way through because it tells how these products act on left-over food and make easy work of what looks like such messy problems. This is essential background for making the most important decision of all—choosing the right product.

Washing Dishes By Hand

There are six steps. As you can see, they are very simple—but very important. Small things make a difference here—tips on how to proceed in an organized, orderly manner. Follow the order suggested here for a few days, and the routine will become second nature to you.

Before you start, run your eye down Chart 5.2 (Hand Dishwashing Supplies) Page 149. This is just a reminder of what you will need.

Now the six steps.

- *Prepare the dishwater.* Fill the sink or dishpan with water that is comfortably hot to your hands. As you do this, add one long squirt of a light-duty liquid detergent such as Dawn, Ivory Liquid, or Joy. Swish the water to disperse the product.

- *Organize the items* so you can wash the least soiled first, the most soiled last. In this order:

  1. glasses and cups
  2. flatware, including knives, forks, spoons

3. plates used for eating
4. serving dishes
5. casseroles or baking dishes
6. pots, pans, heavily soiled utensils.

- *Wash the items.* As you wash the items mentioned above, you may see the water gradually become greasy or dirty. Use your good judgment about changing the washwater. Otherwise, the items at the bottom of the list might not get properly cleaned.

- *Rinse with hot water.* The best way is to hold the dishes under water running from the faucet. If you are trying to conserve water (when there is a drought, for instance), fill up a dishpan and dip the dishes in. This way, you rinse suds off dishes into the water, so it must be changed now and then.

- *Drain.* Dishes can be drained in a draining rack or on a towel which can be placed on a sink drainboard, or on a counter next to the sink.

- *Dry the items.* Dishes can be air-dried or towel-dried. Air drying is more sanitary because the dishes are handled less. On the other hand, glassware and flatware will sparkle more when dried by towel because all traces of water droplets will be buffed away. The towel must be absolutely clean, of course, or it will leave deposits.

As easy as all this looks, there are special problems that can complicate things. Chart 5.3 (Hand Dishwashing Problems . . . Causes and Solutions) Pages 150-151 can probably tell you exactly what to do.

Using An Automatic Dishwasher

If you have an automatic dishwasher, you know what a blessing it can be. But there are rules to follow for correct use, and a price to pay if you ignore them.

5/How to Plan Better Dishwashing

- *Remove excess food.* Scrape away excess food and soil from dishes before putting them in the dishwasher. This will give you a much better cleaning job. If you don't, you run the risk that some bits of soil will remain on a dish through the washing process and will dry as spots or streaks.

- *Know your materials.* Not every pot and pan should be washed in an automatic dishwasher. And some that can be should be placed away from the detergent dispenser. All of this information is spelled out in Chart 5.4 (Cleaning Dishwashable Items) Pages 152-161. Right now, take just a minute to read it. In the future, when you buy a new utensil, consult this chart to see whether it can be washed in the dishwasher.

- *Load dishes correctly.* Soiled surfaces should face toward the water source and be tilted to help the water drain off. Make sure the items are secure in the rack, not loose where the water jet might bounce them around and crack or break them. And it's best not to crowd items because that might keep the water from reaching the entire surface of some items. It is always smart to read and follow the instructions given by the manufacturer of the dishwasher.

- *Use the right product.* When the dishwasher is loaded, fill the automatic dispenser with detergent. Using the right product is always important, but never more so than here. It must be a detergent made specifically for automatic dishwashers. Cascade is an example. Non-dishwasher detergents produce too much suds, and that means poor results—streaks, spots, a general mess.

- *Select the cycle.* The best advice is to read the manufacturer's instructions carefully, then select the right cycle for the kind of load you want to do. Here are some examples: regular/normal cycle for typical daily loads; short/light cycle for lightly soiled dishes or small loads; rinse-and-hold cycle when you want to rinse a partial load and hold it over until the dishwasher is full. Dishwashers differ, so follow the written instructions.

One of the best ways to get the most out of your automatic dishwasher, and spare yourself a headache or two, is to make yourself aware of the problems that might come up and how to prevent them. Chart 5.5 (Dishwasher Problems . . . Causes, Solutions, Preventive Measures) Pages 162-169, probably answers every question you will ever have. If not, look for a toll-free telephone number on the manufacturer's literature or the detergent package, and describe the problem in detail. Everybody wants you to enjoy your automatic dishwasher, and to help make it the blessing you expect it to be.

Chapter 5

Related Charts

Chart 5.1   Dishwashing Products and Aids
Chart 5.2   Hand Dishwashing Supplies
Chart 5.3   Hand Dishwashing Problems ... Causes and Solutions
Chart 5.4   Cleaning Dishwashable Items
Chart 5.5   Dishwasher Problems ... Causes, Solutions, Preventive Measures

Dishwashing Products and Aids

PRODUCT CLASSIFICATION	AVAILABLE FORMS*	RECOMMENDED USE
DISHWASHING DETERGENTS **Light Duty**	Liquid—(Dawn) (Ivory Liquid) (Joy)	Designed for handwashing tableware and cookware. Can also be used for hand laundering lightly soiled lingerie and delicate fabrics. Be sure products containing chlorine bleach and liquid detergents are diluted before using them together. If these products are mixed full strength, noxious fumes can result.
Automatic Dishwashing	Granular (Cascade) Liquid (Cascade)	Designed specifically for washing tableware and cookware in an automatic dishwasher. NO OTHER TYPE OF PRODUCT SHOULD EVER BE USED IN THE DISHWASHER IN PLACE OF AN AUTOMATIC DISHWASHING DETERGENT.

*(Procter & Gamble products)

Chart 5.1

GENERAL INFORMATION

PERSONAL NOTES

Certain characteristics are important in a hand dishwashing liquid: lasting suds, effective cleaning performance, mildness to hands, safety for dishes and other washables, storage stability, pleasant fragrance and appearance, convenient packaging and dispensing.

Usage is often based on the amount it takes to produce a rich, thick layer of suds. An important difference in the quantity of liquid dishwashing detergent required is the concentration of the ingredients vs. water in a product. More concentrated products are more efficient and may be more economical to use than the more dilute ones.

In theory, any detergent can be used for hand dishwashing except an automatic dishwashing detergent. However, many laundry detergents are not very acceptable, particularly a low or no phosphate formula which 1) may leave spots and streaks, 2) may not completely dissolve if a granular type or 3) may discolor certain metals with soaking. A well-formulated, laundry detergent may be the choice for dishwashing in some economy-minded homes, but for most, a light duty liquid dishwashing detergent is the best choice.

Automatic dishwashing detergents provide the chemical energy needed to remove food soil from all types of cooking and serving items. These detergents must be very low to nonsudsing, since suds would cushion the mechanical cleaning action of the water. In addition, they should also inhibit foam that certain protein-containing foods, such as egg and milk, create. Automatic dishwashing detergents must also soften water to prevent insoluble deposits, loosen and hold soil in suspension, leave items clean and grease free so they rinse and dry without spots, and be safe for a wide variety of materials.

(Continued)

Dishwashing Products and Aids *(Continued)*

PRODUCT CLASSIFICATION	AVAILABLE FORMS	RECOMMENDED USE
DISHWASHING AIDS		
Specialty Products	Granular	Designed to remove a build-up of hard water film and cloudiness on dishes and the interior of the dishwasher. Can be used separately or along with the automatic dishwashing detergent. Follow manufacturer's instructions.
	Liquid	Designed to remove lime and rust deposits from the interior of the dishwasher. The product is added at the beginning of the main wash cycle (no dishes or other product present) with the dishwasher completing the rest of the cycle automatically. The dishwasher should then be put through another complete cycle using a dishwashing detergent to clean the interior of any dissolved lime or rust residue.
Rinse Agents	Liquid Solid	Products designed to lower the surface tension of water in the dishwasher so it sheets off dishes rather than drying as droplets, thus helping to eliminate spotting.

Chart 5.1

GENERAL INFORMATION

Some dishwasher manufacturers suggest using white vinegar or chlorine bleach to remove film and stains. When using any product not specifically made for dishwasher use, follow the dishwasher manufacturer's instructions precisely and do not substitute or vary the procedures. Make certain the product is safe for the item being cleaned.

Liquids are available for use in dishwashers with a rinse agent reservoir and dispenser; a solid form is made to hang on the dishwasher rack where it slowly dissolves into each water change in the cycle.

Rinse agents are more helpful in hard or high solids water areas. In soft and moderately hard water areas, increasing the amount of the automatic dishwashing detergent is an effective way to handle water hardness, thus improve spotting and filming performance.

PERSONAL NOTES

Hand Dishwashing Supplies — Chart 5.2

Bottle Brush	Available in different sizes; a great help in getting into deep items like bottles, tall glasses, etc.
Dish Drainer	Plastic coated—permits orderly stacking of rinsed dishes and facilitates air drying.
Dish Towels	Keep spotlessly clean.
Dishcloth or Sponge	Some prefer a cloth. Some prefer a sponge. Whichever is used, make sure it is clean.
Dishpan	Plastic pans help protect against dish/glass breakage.
Drainboard	Plastic drain trays protect sink drainboard or counter top and also protect dishes from breakage on hard surfaces.
Plastic Scrubbers	Very desirable for scouring anything that scratches easily such as Teflon-lined pans, highly polished metal, or china.
Rubber or Plastic Spatulas	Great for scraping dishes and pans before washing.
Silverware Drainer	Keeps flatware together, helps protect it and facilitates air drying.
Sink Mat	Desirable to help prevent breakage if sink is used for dishwashing instead of a dishpan.
Sink Stopper	Essential if sink is used for dishwashing and the sink drain is not equipped with a built-in stopper.
Steel Wool Pads	Good for tough scouring jobs on durable surfaces. The soap-filled pads are excellent for polishing aluminum and stainless steel pans.

Hand Dishwashing Problems... Causes and Solutions*

PROBLEMS	CAUSES
Gray or metal marks on dinnerware.	Knife or fork drawn across the surface of some types of dinnerware, generally the stronger, harder ceramic materials. A spoon used to stir in a stoneware cup.
Spots and film on glassware.	Wash water temperature too low. Insufficient amount of detergent.
Burned-on food in pans.	Cooking at too high a temperature or too long a time.
Baked-on food in casseroles, other bakeware of glass or glass-ceramic material.	Cooking certain types of food such as those containing cheese, gravies, eggs or pie fillings.
Coffee, tea stains on plastic or china cups.	Cups not rinsed and washed soon after using.
Darkened aluminum.	Exposure to certain minerals and alkalies in some foods and water.
Staining of nonstick cookware.	Minerals in water, baked-on fat food stains or the use of excessive heat.

*Developed by The Consumer Affairs Committee of The Soap and Detergent Association

Chart 5.3

SOLUTIONS

Scour gently with baking soda, a mild abrasive cleanser or plastic mesh pad.

Same as above.

Increase water temperature and rinse thoroughly in hot water.

Increase amount of detergent.

Bring a solution of water and liquid detergent to a boil in the pan, simmer until soil loosens; or soak overnight. Or, scrub with baking soda (not on aluminum, however); rinse and dry.

Soak overnight in detergent and water solution. In extreme cases, a little automatic dishwashing detergent in hot water will loosen soil after a short soaking. For scouring, use baking soda, an abrasive cleanser or a specially manufactured product. Do not use metal scouring pads as they may scratch the surface.

Use a special cleaner made for coffee pots and cups, or a solution of 1 tablespoon (15 ml) liquid or powdered chlorine bleach in 1 quart (0.95 L) of water. Certain oxygen bleaches can be used. Follow label directions.

Another method is to wash cups in a solution of 3 tablespoons (45 ml) baking soda to 1 quart (0.95 L) of hot water or shake baking soda into a damp cloth or sponge, rub surface until clean, rinse and dry.

Avoid the use of an abrasive cleanser which may abrade the surface and make the cups more subject to stains.

Boil a solution of 2-3 tablespoons (30-45 ml) of cream of tartar, lemon juice or vinegar to 1 quart (0.95 L) of water in the utensil for 5-10 minutes. Then lightly scour with a steel wool soap pad.

Cooking an acid food such as tomatoes will also remove the stains and will not affect the food.

Clean with a metal cleaning product recommended for use on aluminum. Follow package directions.

Use any **one** of the following solutions:
  To 1 qt. (0.95 L) of water, add ¼ cup (60 ml) coffee pot cleaner. **Or**
  to 1 cup (240 ml) of water, add 3 tablespoons (45 ml) of oxygen bleach. **Or**
  to 1 cup (240 ml) of water, add 3 tablespoons (45 ml) automatic dishwashing detergent.
Let the solution simmer in the stained pan for 15-20 minutes. Wash the pan thoroughly, rinse and dry. Then recondition the pan with cooking oil or shortening before using.

To prevent staining, use the lowest heat that will do the job.

Cleaning Dishwashable Items

SURFACE	END USE	CARE PROCEDURES
Aluminum	Bakeware Cookware	Can be washed in the dishwasher, but should be placed away from the detergent dispenser where undissolved product could come in direct contact with items being washed. For darkened pans, scour with soap impregnated, fine steel wool pads. For severe darkening, simmer an acid food or 2-3 tablespoons of cream of tartar, lemon juice or vinegar per quart of water in the pan for 5-10 minutes. Rinse and polish with soap impregnated steel wool pads. Wash, rinse and dry. Or clean with a metal cleaning product recommended for use on aluminum. Follow package instructions.
Anodized Aluminum	Bakeware available without color Cookware available with or without color	Anodized aluminum without color can be washed in the dishwasher. Colored anodized aluminum may lose the color if washed in the dishwasher.
Cast Iron	Cookware	Wash by hand in hot, sudsy water. Rinse and dry. Utensil will rust if not thoroughly dried or properly seasoned. To Season: Coat pan with unsalted fat or cooking oil and heat in a warm oven (250°F or 121°C) for several hours.
China	Ashtrays Dinnerware Figurines Vases	Obtain care instructions when purchasing china, especially regarding washing in an automatic dishwasher. Underglaze decorated dinnerware is generally dishwasher safe. Overglaze decorations are more likely to show some fading. Use an automatic dishwashing detergent carrying the Seal of Approval of the American Fine China Guild (e.g., Cascade). Use at least the recommended amount of detergent to provide protection for dinnerware patterns (extra detergent will give added protection).

Chart 5.4

SPECIAL INFORMATION

Avoid prolonged periods of soaking with water or acid foods to help prevent pitting.

Aluminum darkening is caused by exposure to certain minerals and alkalies in some foods and water. Avoid the use of ammonia and baking soda which also causes darkening.

Colored anodized aluminum should not be used in an oven. Avoid scouring with a cleanser.

Avoid 1) washing in an automatic dishwasher, 2) prolonged soaks and 3) scouring the interior of the utensil. These procedures will remove the seasoning and cause rusting.

Hand painted or antique china should not be washed in the dishwasher.

When stacking dishes, use protective pads between plates to minimize scratching. Sharp knives and other utensils can scratch the china, too.

Avoid using scouring pads or abrasive cleansers.

Handle china gently whether washing by hand or in an automatic dishwasher.

PERSONAL NOTES

(Continued)

Cleaning Dishwashable Items *(Continued)*

SURFACE	END USE	CARE PROCEDURES
(China) *(Continued)*		Empty coffee and tea from cups soon after using. If the cups are stained, soak in a solution of a dishwashing detergent containing bleach, such as Cascade, or in a chlorine bleach solution. Wash and rinse thoroughly.
Copper	Bottom finish on stainless steel cookware	Wash in a detergent solution, rinse and towel dry.
	Cookware Decorative objects	Use a special copper cleaner (available in grocery stores) to restore darkened copper to a bright finish.
Earthenware	Casual dinnerware	Wash in an automatic dishwasher or wash by hand in a hot sudsy solution. Rinse.
Glass	*Borosilicate glass* Bakeware Coffee makers Cookware Microwave cookware	Wash in an automatic dishwasher, positioning glasses as recommended by the dishwasher manufacturer. Or wash by hand in hot sudsy water and rinse. Towel dry for most spotless film-free results.
	Lead glass Crystal Cut glass	After washing, lead glass may be polished by rubbing with crumpled tissue paper.
	Lime glass Drinking glasses Jars Milk bottles Vases	
Glass Ceramics	*Glazed* Tableware	Wash by hand or in the automatic dishwasher.
	Unglazed Bakeware Broilware Cookware Freezer storage Microwave cookware	

Chart 5.4

SPECIAL INFORMATION

Most baked clay dinnerware has a glazed surface fired on the dish to reduce absorbency, protect colors and designs, and enhance appearance. Glazes differ in composition, hardness, and firing temperatures. The most protection is given by glazes fired at the highest temperatures. China and stoneware are fired at high temperatures, thus are the hardest and most durable of the dinnerware. Earthenware and pottery are fired at lower temperatures and are porous and chip easily.

Copper darkens in use or just with exposure to air. Items often have an anti-tarnish lacquer which should be removed if articles are to be heated.

To remove anti-tarnish lacquer submerge copper in a solution of baking soda and boiling water; let stand until water has cooled; peel off lacquer; wash, rinse and towel dry.

Earthenware, fired at low temperatures, is porous and chips easily. Food soils will be absorbed where the glaze is broken.

To restore cloudy, streaked, spotted or filmed glassware (usually caused by hard water), soak in a dilute vinegar solution (½ cup per gallon of water). Follow with a hot detergent wash. Rinse.

To Remove Spots and Film With a Vinegar Treatment in the Automatic Dishwasher: Wash and rinse load as usual. Remove all metal items (pans, silverware, etc.). Place 2 cups of white vinegar in a container on the bottom rack. Run dishwasher through a complete washing cycle.

Permanent etching of glassware can occur in time with automatic dishwasher care, especially in softened or naturally soft water. Use of the recommended amount of detergent is important to minimize etching.

Use only soft abrasive products for removing heavy soil.

PERSONAL NOTES

(Continued)

Cleaning Dishwashable Items *(Continued)*

SURFACE	END USE	CARE PROCEDURES
Non-Stick Finishes (Some examples are: Teflon®, Silverstone®, Xylan®, etc.)	Bakeware Cookware	Wash either by hand in hot detergent solution or in an automatic dishwasher. Wash thoroughly after each use to prevent buildup of grease and other food soils. If food residues do build up causing staining, use a special cleaner for non-stick finishes (available in grocery, hardware or department stores). Follow package instructions. Or use any ONE of the following solutions: —To 1 qt. (0.95 L) of water, add ¼ cup (60 ml) coffee pot cleaner **Or** —To 1 cup (240 ml) of water, add 3 tablespoons (45 ml) of oxygen bleach **Or** —To 1 cup (240 ml) of water, add 3 tablespoons (45 ml) automatic dishwashing detergent. Let the solution simmer in the stained pan for 15-20 minutes. Wash the pan thoroughly, rinse and dry. Then recondition the pan with cooking oil or shortening before using. To prevent staining, use the lowest heat that will do the job.
Pewter	Bowls Dinner plates Drinkware Pitchers Vases	Wash frequently by hand in hot sudsy water and polish.
Plastics	*Thermoplastic* Disposable dinnerware Disposable drinkware Drinkware Freezer cartons Storage cartons	Wash by hand in hot sudsy water or if recommended by the manufacturer, wash in an automatic dishwasher.
	Thermosetting Dinnerware Handles on cookware and bakeware Microwave cookware	Wash by hand in hot sudsy water or wash in an automatic dishwasher. Although all plastic cookware labeled for microwave use can be washed in the dishwasher, follow manufacturer's instructions. Some items can be placed in either the top or bottom racks. Others should be placed in the top rack only.

Chart 5.4

SPECIAL INFORMATION

Avoid using abrasive cleansers or scouring pads. Instead, use plastic scrubbers or nylon net.

Avoid using sharp or rough-edged kitchen cooking utensils to minimize scratching the non-stick finish.

Do not wash in the automatic dishwasher.

Avoid using abrasive cleansers or scouring pads.

Avoid scratching with sharp knives. Do not use abrasive cleansers or scouring pads.

Thermosetting plastics, such as Melamine, and all thermoplastic items should not be used in conventional ovens, top of the range cooking or broiling. Follow manufacturer's instructions for microwave plastics. Look for statements like "For Microwave Cooking Only," "Suitable For Conventional or Microwave Oven," and other similar permanent markings.

To remove stains, soak in an automatic dishwashing detergent (3 tablespoons per 1 cup water) or a solution of chlorine bleach, following package instructions.

PERSONAL NOTES

(Continued)

Cleaning Dishwashable Items *(Continued)*

SURFACE	END USE	CARE PROCEDURES
Porcelain Enamel	Bakeware Cookware Mugs Plates	Wash in a sudsy detergent solution and rinse. Or wash in the automatic dishwasher.
Pottery	Bowls Dinnerware	Wash in a sudsy detergent solution and rinse. Or wash in the automatic dishwasher.
Silverplate	Candle bases Flatware Tableware Trays	Wash and/or rinse all silverplate promptly to prevent tarnish, staining or pitting by food soils. Wash by hand in a sudsy detergent solution. Rinse and dry to polish. Or wash in the dishwasher positioning items, especially flatware, so they do not touch stainless steel. (Remember most silver knives have stainless steel blades.) Electrolytic action between silverplate and stainless steel can cause pitting of the stainless.
Stainless Steel	Bakeware Candle bases Cookware Flatware Tableware Trays	See care procedures and special information for silverplate. For heavily soiled/stained areas, use a stainless steel cleaner, following package instructions. Or scour with a soap impregnated steel wool pad.

Chart 5.4

SPECIAL INFORMATION

Avoid scouring with an abrasive cleanser.

The enamel can chip or craze if dropped or exposed to sudden temperature changes, producing areas where rusting can occur.

Pottery is clayware fired at lower temperatures than earthenware and is porous and chips easily.

Pottery is unsanitary if food soils are allowed to be absorbed where the glaze is damaged.

Using an electroplating process, silverplate is produced by coating a nonprecious metal (brass, copper, nickel silver or stainless steel) with a layer of pure silver. Better grades of silverplate have a thicker layer of silver and sometimes a double thickness at wear points (base of spoon bowl).

Avoid letting undiluted liquid dishwashing detergents or undissolved automatic dishwashing detergents from coming into direct contact with silverplate.

Avoid washing antique silverplate or hollow handled knives in the dishwasher. Knife handles may loosen in the dishwasher.

Remove tarnish by using a silverpolish, following the package instructions. Minimize tarnish by cleaning with a tarnish inhibitor or store in a tarnish-proof drawer or chest. Securing silverplate with rubber bands will increase tarnish.

Stainless steel is an alloy of iron, carbon, chromium or chromium/nickel and traces of other metals. Kinds and percentages of these elements can be varied to provide differing degrees of corrosion resistance, hardness, ductility, buffing properties and ability to hold a cutting edge.

Stainless steel does not tarnish. However, it can be stained or pitted by prolonged exposure to salty or acid foods (fruits, fruit juices, salad dressings, vinegar, milk).

Discoloration can be minimized by using low to medium instead of high heat.

PERSONAL NOTES

(Continued)

Cleaning Dishwashable Items *(Continued)*

SURFACE	END USE	CARE PROCEDURES
Sterling Silver	Candle bases Flatware Tableware Trays	See care procedures and special information for silverplate.
Stoneware	Dinnerware Tableware	Wash in an automatic dishwasher or wash by hand in hot sudsy solution. Rinse.
Wood	Cutting boards Dinnerware Drinkware Knife handles Mixing spoons Salad bowls Tableware Trays	Wash by hand quickly in hot sudsy water. Rinse immediately and dry thoroughly before putting away. Do not wash in the dishwasher unless recommended by the manufacturer.

Chart 5.4

SPECIAL INFORMATION

Sterling silver is a precious metal and by U.S. Standards must be 92.5 parts silver to 7.5 parts alloy (for hardness). Frequent use retards tarnish and develops a soft, lustrous appearance.

Stoneware, fired at a high temperature, is nonporous and nonabsorbent.

Wood is porous and will absorb moisture causing it to warp, crack, fade and produce a rough surface upon drying.

Do not soak wood items.

Untreated or unfinished cutting boards and wooden kitchen spoons are likely to stain. Since sanitation is more important than appearance, these items can be scoured with a stiff brush, bleached, or even put in the dishwasher, though this will shorten their life.

PERSONAL NOTES

Dishwasher Problems . . . Causes, Solutions, Preventive Measures*

PROBLEMS

Spotting/filming/ poor cleaning results.

CAUSES

Insufficient amount of detergent.

Hard water.

Water temperature too low.

Improper loading.

Insufficient water fill.

Filter needs cleaning.

*Developed by The Consumer Affairs Committee of The Soap and Detergent Association

Chart 5.5

SOLUTIONS	PREVENTIVE MEASURES
Increase the amount of detergent, especially when washing full loads or in hard water, or when using the "energy-saving" cycle or "air/no-heat" drying.	Use sufficient amount of detergent.
Use additional detergent and a rinse agent or both.	Use sufficient amount of detergent and a rinse agent.

To remove heavy, cloudy, hard water film from utensils, use any one of the following solutions:
    Stripping product according to package directions. Or
    white vinegar, chlorine bleach then white vinegar. Or
    citric acid crystals.
Follow the dishwasher manufacturer's instructions precisely. Remove flatware or other metal items from the dishwasher when using white vinegar, chlorine bleach or citric acid crystals.
	In extremely hard water areas, installation of a water softener may be necessary.

Set water heater at 140°F (60°C). Run dishwasher when other household demands for hot water (such as for laundry or bathing) are low.	Same as solution.
Follow dishwasher manufacturer's instructions for proper loading procedures. Place dishes so water spray reaches all soiled surfaces. Do not overcrowd the bottom rack since this will block the water spray.	Same as solution.
Water pressure may be low. Do not use water for any other purposes while dishwasher is in operation.	Same as solution.
Check service manual for water pressure recommendations or call appliance service company.	Same as solution.
Remove any accumulated or deposited foods.	If dishwasher has a filter, check and clean filter periodically.

(Continued)

Dishwasher Problems... Causes, Solutions, Preventive Measures *(Continued)*

PROBLEMS	CAUSES
Spotting/filming/ poor cleaning results. (Continued)	Oversudsing— Prewashing with a liquid dishwashing detergent.
	Insufficient amount of detergent.
Small particles (food or detergent) left on items.	Water not reaching surfaces, dishwasher overcrowded.
	Water temperature too low.
	Insufficient water fill.
	Detergent stored too long or under adverse conditions.
Detergent cakes in dispenser cup.	Dampness in cup.
	Faulty cover.
	Improper loading.
	Old detergent.
Dark spots on sterling or silverplate items.	Contact of wet items with undissolved or highly concentrated detergent.

Chart 5.5

SOLUTIONS	PREVENTIVE MEASURES
Rinse items thoroughly before putting them in the dishwasher to remove liquid dishwashing detergent.	Use "rinse-hold" cycle on dishwasher, or rinse thoroughly. (Note: It should not be necessary to prewash dishes.)
Increase amount of detergent to inhibit suds caused by protein soils and washing action.	Same as solution.
Check to be sure water action is not blocked by dishes. Check filter for accumulated or deposited food or detergent.	Load dishwasher correctly. Keep filter clean.
Set water heater at 140°F (60°C)	Same as solution.
Water pressure may be low. Do not use water for any other purposes while dishwasher is in operation.	Same as solution.
Check service manual for water pressure recommendations or call appliance service company.	Same as solution.
Use detergent within one-two months after purchase. Open one box at a time. Always close pouring spout after each use. Store in a cool, dry place.	Same as solution.
Make sure cup is dry before adding detergent and start dishwasher immediately.	Same as solution.
Do not overfill. Cover should close tightly. Check cover for fit. It may need to be repaired or replaced.	Same as solution.
Do not place large items such as platters in front of cups.	Same as solution.
Use detergent within one-two months of purchase.	To assure freshness, buy detergent as needed and no more than one or two at a time.
Remove spots with silver polish. Rewash.	Do not overload silverware basket.
	Avoid spilling detergent directly on flatware. Make sure dispenser cup is properly closed, and close dishwasher door slowly. If possible, move silverware basket away from dispenser cup.

(Continued)

Dishwasher Problems . . . Causes, Solutions, Preventive Measures *(Continued)*

PROBLEMS	CAUSES
Pitting of stainless steel items.	Prolonged contact with salty or highly acid foods.
	Contact of wet items with undissolved or highly concentrated detergent.
	Contact between silver and stainless steel in dishwasher.
Bronze tarnish on silverplate.	Silverplate is worn off.
Discoloration of aluminum.	Exposure to certain minerals and alkalies in some foods and water plus high drying temperature.
Black or gray marks on dishes.	Aluminum utensils rubbing against dishes.
Chipping and breakage of dishes/glasses.	Improper loading.

Chart 5.5

SOLUTIONS	PREVENTIVE MEASURES
Remove spots with silver polish. Rewash.	Wash soon after use or rinse (use "rinse-hold" cycle) if items are not to be washed right away.
Same as above.	Do not overload silverware basket.
	Avoid spilling detergent directly on flatware. Make sure dispenser cup is properly closed, and close dishwasher door slowly. If possible, move silverware basket away from dispenser cups.
Same as above.	Place silver and stainless steel flatware in silverware basket so they do not touch. Most silver knives have stainless steel blades; make sure knives are all placed with blades in same direction.
A temporary solution is to soak the flatware in vinegar for 10 minutes. Rinse and dry. The permanent solution is to replate the silver.	Replate the silver. Check manufacturer's directions on "dishwashability" of silverplate.
Boil a solution of 2-3 tablespoons (30-45 ml) of cream of tartar, lemon juice or vinegar to 1 quart (0.95 L) of water in the utensil for 5-10 minutes. Then lightly scour with a steel wool soap pad. Clean with a metal cleaning product recommended for use on aluminum. Follow package directions. Cooking an acid food such as tomatoes will also remove the stains and will not affect the food.	If water is causing the discoloration, do not use dry cycle or remove aluminumware after the final rinse.
Remove marks with a plastic scouring pad and a mild cleanser.	Be sure dishes and aluminum utensils do not rub against each other in the dishwasher. ?This is particularly important with the lightweight foil containers.
Irreversible condition.	Load with care following the dishwasher manufacturer's instructions. Place glassware so it does not touch other pieces. Remove from dishwasher carefully.

(Continued)

Dishwasher Problems... Causes, Solutions, Preventive Measures *(Continued)*

PROBLEMS	CAUSES
Distortion of plastics.	Plastics vary in their tolerance to heat.
Dishes not dry.	Water temperature too low.
	Improper loading.
	Use of "air/no-heat" drying option.
Damage to delicate and miscellaneous items, such as colored anodized aluminum, pewter, cast iron, antique or hand painted china, wood.	Some items are not dishwasher safe.
Yellow or brown stains on dishes and/or dishwasher interior.	Iron or manganese content in water supply.
Iridescence/coating or film/etching of glassware.	A water or chemical reaction with some glassware. Usually caused by some combination of soft or softened water, alkaline washing solutions reacting with some types of glass. Can be accelerated by poor rinsing, overloading and excessive water temperature.
Odor in dishwasher.	Dishes washed only every two or three days.

Chart 5.5

SOLUTIONS	PREVENTIVE MEASURES
Irreversible condition.	Always check the washing instructions for plastic items to be sure they are dishwasher safe. Load plastics in top rack and away from heating element located in the bottom of dishwasher. Handwash extremely heat-sensitive plastic items.
Set water heater at 140°F (60°C).	Same as solution.
Load so all items are properly tilted for good drainage. Avoid nesting of dishes and/or silverware.	Same as solution.
Use of a rinse agent will aid in drying.	Same as solution.
Irreversible condition.	DO NOT put these items in the dishwasher unless recommended by the manufacturer. Check instruction booklet first.
After food soil is removed, wash dishes with citric acid crystals. Check dishwasher manufacturer's instructions for amount to use and method. Do not add detergent. A liquid product is available to remove iron deposits from the dishwasher interior; follow package directions.	To retard staining, use maximum amount of dishwasher detergent to keep iron or manganese in suspension during the wash and use a rinse additive during the rinse. If staining cannot be controlled, the only solution is the installation of iron removal equipment in the home water supply.
Irreversible condition.	The condition may not always be preventable. To minimize the possibility of etching, use a minimum of detergent, but not less than 1 tablespoon (15 ml). Set water heater no higher than 140°F (60°C), underload dishwasher for thorough rinsing and draining, and dry without heat. Use of a rinse agent may also help.
Use the "rinse-hold" cycle at least once a day until a load accumulates.	Same as solution.

6 The Consumer and P&G... Creating the Right Product Together

One of the main themes of this book is that nothing is more important than choosing the right product for the job.

But how does the right product come to be, in the first place?

Ask that question of Procter & Gamble, which makes scores of consumer products, and you get the same answer today you would have gotten a hundred years ago. "We listen to consumers. They tell us their problems. That is how everything starts. If many consumers tell us the same thing, we know there is a genuine problem. That is when we go to the laboratory and start the long process of creating a product to solve the problem."

Some people think it works the other way around: A manufacturer makes a product and tries to create consumer demand by heavy advertising. Not so at Procter & Gamble. You can arouse curiosity that way, and some shoppers will give the product a try. But unless it solves a definite problem, history shows the consumer is too smart to stay with it.

Consumers have stayed with many P&G products, not just for years, but for decades. Ivory Soap goes back a hundred years, and then some. So listening to the consumer has a long history at the company... and plays a bigger role than ever in the key steps P&G takes in developing a new product or improving an old one.

The How To Clean Handbook

HOW A PRODUCT IS DEVELOPED

- **Step 1:** Identify Consumer Habits and Needs
- **Step 2:** Determine Type of Product Needed
- **Step 3:** Invent a Product, Determine How to Produce It
- **Step 4:** Develop and Test A Prototype of The Product
- **Step 5:** Improve and Re-test The Product Prototype
- **Step 6:** Finalize The Product
- **Step 7:** Test Consumers' Reaction To The Final Product
- **Step 8:** Develop Product Advertising and Promotion
- **Step 9:** Begin Selling the Product

Finding the consumer's need comes first—Step 1. Not merely finding it, but defining it in every detail, so when it eventually reaches the scientific group who will create a new product the chances of hitting the target squarely will be high. Researchers talk to thousands of individuals. What products do they use? What types of soils are they trying to clean? How much product do they use? What about water temperatures? How much laundry are they loading in their washers?

Facts are important, but so are opinions. Why do consumers buy a certain laundry detergent, for example? What do they like and dislike about this product? What do they know about competing brands? What product changes would they like to see? What do they think the ideal product would be like?

The idea behind getting an exact picture of the consumers' habits and practices is that it is easier to create a product to fit consumers' habits than to change those habits to fit the company's products.

While this rather formalized research is going on, other kinds of fact-finding are in progress, too. One of the most interesting is the information gained from consumer calls reaching P&G on its toll-free "800" telephone lines. The Company receives over half a million phone calls a year, and considers this information along with that gained from consumer letters a treasure. All data is passed along to people at all levels in the company to help keep everybody up-to-date on what consumers are saying and what questions they are asking.

Now comes Step 2 in the product development cycle. All of the research information is analyzed and a composite picture of consumers' habits and practices is pieced together. This picture reveals the current unfilled needs of the consumer, and points to an opportunity for the company to respond by developing a new product or product improvement.

It is at this stage, Step 3, that P&G applies its scientific expertise. With a product opportunity in precise focus, the scientists invent the product formulation and the process for making it. This is called identifying the technology.

Meeting the consumer's needs and wants is one challenge. But there are others. The product must be safe—for the people who make the product, consumers who use it and consumers

Safety is a major concern at Procter & Gamble.

who might misuse it; safe for the environment; and safe for the clothes or floors or dishes or other materials that will be cleaned with the product.

Safety is a major concern at Procter & Gamble. When scientists in the laboratory formulate a new product, they take into account the effect the product will have on everything it touches as it proceeds through factories, stores, homes, down the drain and into the total environment.

In Step 4, the first product prototypes are unveiled. These are in crude form. The main concern at this point is to see whether the basic idea behind the product looks promising enough to carry the process further. The best of, perhaps, many prototypes are then refined, and eventually given to employees and small groups of consumers to test in their homes.

These early versions of the product are tested in plain, black-and-white containers. One reason is the company is not ready to spend money on a finished package until the product proves itself. And it is felt people in the test will make a more objective evaluation if they are not influenced by a brand name, a colorful package, or advertising.

These preliminary tests give the lab experts a chance to check their opinions against the consumers. Does the product work as well for the consumer at home as it does in the lab? Can the consumer see how this product is different and better? If not, it is back to the drawing board for the scientists.

Steps 5 and 6 involve further testing with consumers. As these users report their experiences with the product, Procter & Gamble weighs these new facts and opinions, refines the product, then tests it again.

Different research techniques are used. To find out how well a product removes stains, for example, the company stains pieces of cloth, asks consumers to use the product to wash the stain away in their homes, then return the material so the lab can evaluate the results. Sometimes consumers are asked to wear and wash T-shirts or dress shirts and return them for the company to check on whiteness performance. Panelists enjoy these at-home experiments, and are careful to follow directions to the letter.

One dishwashing project alone involved 4,000 consumers who washed over 100,000 loads of dishes over a period of a year.

In addition, over 1000 loads of dirty clothes are brought to product-testing laundries at P&G every week. Product development personnel apply different product treatments to a wide variety of stains and fabrics, then observe the results firsthand.

All of this testing helps P&G answer these questions that underlie all product development at the company:

1. Is the product benefit, evident in the laboratory, also evident in home use?
2. If so, do consumers notice this benefit? Do they talk about it after the test?
3. If they notice it, are they enthusiastic about it?

The answers to these questions indicate whether the consumer is impressed enough to switch to this new brand. And that, of course, is the ultimate test.

While all this is going on, another consideration is always present: maintaining P&G's reputation for making quality products. The company has rigid specifications for everything, from raw materials to perfumes, and frequent checks (for quality) continue to be made for the rest of the product's life. Since a product may be sold throughout the fifty states, and even abroad, meticulous care is exercised to see that the consumer can count on the same high quality no matter where or when a purchase is made.

When the battery of tests and refinements have produced the final product, Step 7 calls for still more tests.

In one, for example, the company sends samples of the new product to consumers, along with instructions on how to use it. They use the product for a specified period of time. What they have to say is then collected by written questionnaires or telephone interviews.

P&G also believes the scientists who produced the product should have face-to-face conversations with panelists who have tested their creation. They sit down in a room with five to ten users, called focus groups, and talk back and forth about how the product performed, what they liked or disliked, how it compared with competing brands—anything relevant that comes to mind.

All of this information gives P&G a detailed picture of the consumers' habits and practices, needs and wants, and state of mind, all crucial to the development of the marketing plan, which is Step 8 in the cycle.

But, the consumers have not quite finished. There is more testing to be done. Do the consumers find the package convenient to use and store? Would they be willing to pay the proposed price? Are the usage instructions on the package clear, complete, easy to follow? Are the ads and other promotional materials believable, informative, in good taste? These are critical questions, and consumers' opinions are often sought before the marketing plan can be finalized and put into action.

Step 9 is the event all this effort has been leading up to—the debut of the product on store shelves.

But the dialogue with consumers continues. With the toll-free telephone number on every P&G package, consumers have easy access to product information, and a convenient means of telling the company what they like and dislike. All these consumer comments are computerized and the data used to guide the product development technicians in visualizing new products and improvements.

As new trends, new appliances, new lifestyles come on the scene, the laundry, cleaning and dishwashing products that consumers depend on must keep pace. To that end, P&G and consumers carry on their never-ending dialogue.

> **As new trends, new appliances, new lifestyles come on the scene, the laundry, cleaning and dishwashing products that consumers depend on must keep pace.**

7 Frequently Asked Questions (and Their Answers)

The Consumer Services Section of P&G's Public Affairs Division today numbers more than 80 persons who respond to about a million consumer inquiries a year through phone calls and letters. Although some people contact the company about problems, about half of those who write or phone simply want to say they like P&G products or to ask more questions about products or other company matters. Here are some of the kinds of questions P&G gets.

Questions About Laundering

1. *Question:* Can I use any P&G dishwashing or household cleaning products to do my laundry?
   Answer: We do not recommend P&G dishwashing or cleaning products for doing laundry for these reasons:

   Dishwashing Products

   — *Cascade*—It is designed for use in automatic dishwashers and this is the only use we recommend. Cascade contains a small amount of chlorine bleach which could adversely affect non-colorfast dyes if used for laundering fabrics.

— *Joy, Ivory Liquid, Dawn*—Besides handwashing dishes, these products are excellent for handwashing delicate fabrics and for pretreating difficult stains. We do not recommend them for use in washers since they could cause the washer to oversuds. Further, these products do not contain ingredients for cleaning heavily-soiled clothes.

Cleaners and Cleansers

— *Top-Job*—Not recommended for laundry. The green pigment in the product could permanently stain fabric.

— *Comet, Comet Liquid*—Not recommended for laundry. These products contain an abrasive which could damage the fibers. Further, they contain chlorine bleach which could fade some colors.

— *Spic and Span, Spic and Span Pine, Mr. Clean*—Any of these products can be used as a detergent booster by adding 1/2 cup to the washer in addition to your regular laundry detergent. (They cannot be used as a detergent substitute).

2. *Question:* Are your laundry products safe for laundering baby clothing?
Answer: All our products are formulated with the whole family in mind. Our research people have been careful to eliminate ingredients which are known to have the potential to produce allergies and irritation. We anticipate no difficulty in using any of our laundry products for their recommended use in caring for your baby's laundry.

3. *Question:* Can I wash effectively in cold water?
Answer: Only for certain kinds of laundering. For example, cold water is recommended for dark or bright colors that bleed; or to remove protein stains such as blood. It is very important to read the Care Labels on the clothing, as well as the directions on the product package. Bear this in mind: The colder the water, the more difficult it is to clean a wash

7/Frequently Asked Questions (and Their Answers)

load thoroughly. Detergents lose much of their cleaning effectiveness when the water is cold. Their effectiveness is seriously diminished when the water temperature goes below 60 degrees Fahrenheit.

Keep in mind, however, using cold water for rinsing is ideal. Rinsing in cold water not only minimizes wrinkling of permanent press items, but it also conserves water heating energy.

4. *Question:* Can I get away with using less detergent than the package directions say?
Answer: In some cases, perhaps, but you should test your way carefully. A detergent's usage recommendations are carefully worked out and tested to give you the best cleaning performance. Skimping may bring results that will disappoint you. However, somewhat less than the recommended amount of detergent may be used under these conditions:

— very light soil

— small loads of clothes

— reduced water volume

— soft water

On the other hand, *more* than the recommended detergent will be needed for the following conditions:

— very hard water

— heavily soiled clothes

— large loads

— extra water volume in large capacity washers

— reduced wash action or wash time to protect delicate items

— use of warm or cold water wash temperature

For best results, read the directions on each package carefully. And always use a standard measuring cup.

HINT: For information on water hardness in your area, consult your local water company or County Extension Office (in the phone book under U.S. Department of Agriculture).

5. *Question:* How can I remove a blood stain?
   Answer: Blood is a protein-based stain that can be removed with an enzyme product, like Tide, Liquid Tide, Era Plus, Solo, Liquid Bold 3, Liquid Cheer or Biz. Cold water and Ivory Bar Soap are also usually effective in removing blood stains, particularly if the stain is fresh and has not set.

HINT: 1) Rinse the stained area in cold water and rub on Ivory Bar Soap. Rinse again and repeat. 2) If the stain is not completely removed, soak the garment in warm water with an enzyme product. Make sure the item is totally submerged in water. 3) Re-wash the item with detergent containing an enzyme.

Enzymes are naturally-occurring substances, specifically proteins, that act as catalysts—substances that speed up chemical reactions without changing themselves in the process. Enzymes are thus able to break down certain soils, such as blood, gravy or grass stains, into simpler forms that are more easily removed in the wash process. Follow package usage instructions.

6. *Question:* When do I use oxygen bleaches and when chlorine bleaches?
   Answer: Read both the package directions and the garment Care Labels carefully before using either. That's the key. Then, bleach the whole item, not just the stained area. Thus, if bleaching does slightly lighten the color, the color change will be uniform over the whole item.

HINT: If the item is a two-piece dress or suit, bleach both parts.

7/Frequently Asked Questions (and Their Answers)

Oxygen bleaches generally come in dry, powdered form, like Biz, or in a detergent containing bleach, like Oxydol. They are safe for use on most fabrics and colors, when properly used. Oxygen bleaches are milder than liquid chlorine bleaches and work best in hot water or in a soak.

HINT: *Chlorine bleach is a very strong and effective bleach, but must be handled carefully to prevent fabric and color damage such as fading, spotting.*

Whatever type of bleach you use, oxygen or chlorine, always test fabrics for colorfastness. Test an inconspicuous spot first. Here's how: *For chlorine bleach,* mix one tablespoon of bleach with 1/4 cup of water. Apply one drop of this bleach solution on an inconspicuous portion of the fabric. Let stand one minute. Then blot dry with paper towel. If there is no color change, the article can be safely bleached. *For oxygen bleach,* make a solution of one teaspoon of bleach to one cup of hot water. Dip an unexposed portion of the item up and down in the hot solution. If color does not bleed or there is no color change, the product may be used as recommended for laundering or soaking.

7. *Question:* Why bother adding a fabric softener?
Answer: When you are washing fabrics that have become stiff, harsh, or roughened after repeated washings, such as terry cloth towels, fabric softeners can really make a difference. They prevent fabric fibers from gathering together forming rough clumps during drying. They also help control static cling which is particularly important on synthetics and blends. And since fabric softening reduces wrinkling, it makes ironing easier.

8. *Question:* What does it cost to run my washer or dishwasher?
Answer: The only way to get a reliable answer is to ask your local utility company. Figuring the cost of electricity or gas to heat water for your washer is a complicated matter. Energy rates vary from one community to another. Your utility company will explain the details as they apply to you individually. The best we can say is that the cost is only a matter of cents.

If you wonder sometimes whether to save on energy costs by washing in cold water instead of warm or hot, remember this: Detergents don't clean as well in cold water. The results might disappoint you. This is probably not the best way to economize. However, cold water rinsing is always a good idea.

Questions About Cleaning

1. *Question:* Which P&G product can I use to clean my car?
   Answer: The only product P&G markets that is recommended for general use on cars is Mr. Clean. When diluted in a bucket of water (1/4 cup to a gallon), Mr. Clean is safe for all hard surfaces of your automobile. Mr. Clean is not safe for upholstery and carpeting in the interior of the car and should not be used.
   For spot cleaning of auto chrome and whitewall tires use either Comet or Mr. Clean Cleanser.

2. *Question:* Is it OK to mix P&G cleaners and cleansers with bleach?
   Answer: No. Do not mix bleach with any P&G cleaners or cleansers for the following reasons:

   — *Top Job*—Contains ammonia and the label carries a caution not to mix with bleach

   — *Spic and Span, Spic and Span Pine, Mr. Clean and Mr. Clean Cleanser*—Should not be mixed with bleach. As a general rule, P&G does not recommend mixing cleaning products. Sometimes you can cancel out the effectiveness of one of the products or you may create unpleasant fumes.

   — *Comet, Comet Liquid*—They already contain bleach, so mixing would increase bleach levels and odor considerably.

7/Frequently Asked Questions (and Their Answers)

3. *Question:* Can I use Top Job, Mr. Clean, Spic and Span, Spic and Span Pine, on the following:

— Wood?

Answer: Yes, for cleaning *painted* wood. No, for cleaning *unfinished or varnished* wood. For cleaning painted wood, use 1/4 cup of the product in one gallon of warm water.

— No-Wax Floors?

Answer: Yes, all are recommended for use on no-wax floors. P&G recommends 1/4 cup in one gallon warm water.

— Windows/Glass?

Answer: Yes, windows can be cleaned with either concentrated or diluted Mr. Clean, Top Job, Spic and Span, or Spic and Span Pine. They should be rinsed after cleaning. (Comet, Comet Liquid or Mr. Clean Cleanser are too abrasive for glass.)

— Carpets?

Answer: No, Mr. Clean, Top Job, Spic and Span, and Spic and Span Pine are not recommended for this use since the alkalinity of these products may affect the dyes in the carpet or remove the soil guard. This is also true of Comet and Comet Liquid; these are too abrasive for carpets and contain chlorine bleach, which could affect the dyes in the carpet. Mr. Clean Cleanser should not be used, since it also contains an abrasive.

— What about using Comet and Comet Liquid on the above surfaces?

Answer: No. These products are too abrasive for any of the above surfaces.

4. *Question:* What items should I use powdered cleansers on? When should I *not* use them?
   Answer: Because cleansers, such as Comet and Mr. Clean Cleanser, contain a fine abrasive, they are very effective on tough cleaning jobs on such surfaces as porcelain sinks and bathtubs, stainless steel, ceramic tile and fiberglass. These products can also be successfully used on plastic surfaces if appropriate care is observed. To minimize any possibility of abrasive scratching, rub gently as needed and rinse. Cleansers, however, should not be used on:

   — sterling silver or silver plate

   — china

   — highly polished mirror-like finishes

   — non-stick finishes

   — acrylic or baked enamel cookware, clear acrylic plastic faucets and drinkware

   — glass, including tableware, mirrors, windshields, oven glass

   — soft and clear plastics.

Questions About Dishwashing

1. *Question:* How can I get deep coffee stains off pots?
   Answer: Fill with hot water and add one tablespoon of an automatic dishwashing powder like Cascade. Stir to dissolve thoroughly. Soak for 30 minutes, including basket and stem, wash and rinse thoroughly.

   CAUTION: Do not immerse electric coffeemakers in water.

2. *Question:* How can I prevent caking of an automatic dishwasher detergent?

7/Frequently Asked Questions (and Their Answers)

Answer: If the dishwasher detergent is caking, it means it is being stored in a place that is too moist. Keep products in a cool, dry place, and, of course, away from children and pets.

HINT: *Close package spout carefully after each use and store in a cabinet other than one under the sink where heat and humidity can be excessive.*

---

3. *Question:* How can I eliminate spots on glasses washed by hand?
   Answer: Spots on glasses washed by hand can be eliminated by hand-drying. It also helps to use the proper amount of a hand dishwashing liquid detergent, such as Dawn, Ivory Liquid, or Joy and hotter water.
   In the dishwasher, increase the amount of detergent, especially when washing full loads or in hard water. Cascade automatic dishwashing detergent is specially formulated so water will "sheet off," rather than forming droplets that leave spots after drying.

4. *Question:* Is fine china safe with automatic dishwashing detergents?
   Answer: Yes, provided you use a specially formulated dishwashing detergent, such as Cascade which carries the Seal of Approval of the American Fine China Guild. Cascade contains sodium silicate, an ingredient that helps protect fine china patterns, as well as dishwasher parts, from the effects of heat and water. Of course, hand painted or antique china should not be washed in a dishwasher.

5. *Question:* Can hand dishwashing detergents be used in automatic dishwashers?
   Answer: No. Hand dishwashing detergents produce too many suds and will hinder the water action necessary for cleaning. Further, too many suds may cause the dishwasher to overflow. Only use an automatic dishwashing detergent in the machine. Read directions carefully on the detergent package before using it.

Questions About Products

1. *Question:* Are P&G dishwashing and laundry products safe for septic tanks?
   Answer: Yes. All detergents and household cleaning products in normal use are safe for properly operating septic tanks and other waste water treatment systems.

2. *Question:* Why does Procter & Gamble make so many products?
   Answer: Not all consumers want the same products. Therefore, different brands have been developed with different performance characteristics to meet the needs of many different households.

Other Questions

1. *Question:* Why does Procter & Gamble oppose detergent phosphate bans?
   Answer: Procter & Gamble opposes detergent phosphate bans because they have no effect on water quality, they constitute an undesirable limitation on consumer choice and they interfere with the free market ability to use the most cost effective ingredients in consumer products.

   Detergent phosphate bans do not improve water quality because detergent phosphate is only a very small part of the total phosphate entering lakes and streams. Phosphate enters waterways through "nonpoint" sources, such as land runoff and rainfall, and point sources, such as wastewater treatment plants. Most of the phosphate coming into treatment plants is from human waste and food; less than one quarter is from detergents. To improve water quality, wastewater treatment to remove phosphate, and sometimes improved land management to reduce runoff, is necessary. Waste water treatment is the most cost effective method of making a *meaningful* difference in lake water

7/Frequently Asked Questions (and Their Answers)

quality, because it removes phosphorus and other wastes from *all* municipal sources, not just detergents.

We recognize the interest in zero-phosphate detergents, so we have been trying for years to develop an effective substitute for phosphorus. Liquid Tide and our improved non-phosphate powder Tide are examples of this effort, but as good as they are, they are still not as cost effective as our phosphate brands. In areas where phosphate detergents are permitted, people can choose either phosphate or zero-phosphate brands, and as more zero-phosphate brands become available, the average phosphorus in use is decreasing. However, a *majority* of consumers still choose products which contain phosphates because they represent the best value for their laundry needs.

If you have other questions that have not been answered here, call **the toll-free "800" telephone number** *on every Procter & Gamble product package. For a complete list of these toll-free 800-line numbers, see Page 20. One of our specially-trained operators will be available to answer your questions, take your comments and offer suggestions on a host of cleaning-related topics.*

8 A Little Romance

Unlikely as it seems, soap has a romantic past.

Historians speculate that people always have had an instinct for cleanliness. And some wise person recognized, thousands of years ago, the best way to achieve a clean body and clothing was to immerse them in the water of a river or stream. Dirt washed away, leaving the body invigorated and clothing fresh.

And people began to weave legends.

The First Soap

One tale had it that the first primitive kind of soap came into being the same way many great inventions did—by accident.

In the misty past—say, 3,000 years ago—Romans offered animals as burnt offerings to their gods on Sapo Hill. Fat from these animals accumulated on the sacrificial altars and mixed with ashes from the fires. Rain washed this mixture of fat and alkali down the hill to the clay bank of the Tiber River.

The story goes that women found this clay, when rubbed on wet clothes, loosened the dirt with astonishing ease. Unfortunately, the tale does not tell whether the Romans ever figured out what made the clay so magical or how to replenish the supply when it ran out. But Sapo clay also took its place in history.

Some students of the legend believe the word "soap" derives from Sapo.

The French Influence

Hundreds of years went by. Then, between 100 and 200 A.D., a cleaning product was actually created in France. Many people believe this was the first deliberate attempt to develop a product that deserved to be called soap.

A few centuries later, the Spanish made their contribution. They made soap, called Castile, from olive oil and soda. It was enormously expensive, of course, and beyond the purses of most people.

A few more centuries passed, and then came a significant breakthrough. In the late 1700's a French scientist, named Nicolas Leblanc, found that caustic soda, an important soap ingredient, could be made from common table salt. This meant that soap, until now a luxury, could be made and marketed at a price that most people could afford. It would not be long before soap became an indispensable staple in virtually every home, no matter how humble.

Early American Soap

In Colonial America, many a community made good money by exporting ashes and fat to the soap-makers in Europe. And many early settlers made their own soap. They poured hot water over wood ashes to make an alkali called potash. Then they boiled the potash with animal fats to make soap. They poured the soap into large wooden frames for hardening. Then they cut the hardened soap into bars and sold them door-to-door. For laundering, these bars were cut into small pieces or shaved so they would dissolve quickly.

The soap did a fair job. But it was not an unmixed blessing—it was harsh, and the odor horrendous.

One of the most fascinating milestones in soap-making occurred in the early 1800's. Scientists began to appreciate the importance of cleanliness, and people started using hot water extensively, for many purposes. To their surprise and delight, they discovered soap had far more cleaning power in hot water than in cold. The greater effectiveness of hot water was to revolutionize the soap-makers' thinking in their search for better and better products.

Historic improvements lay ahead as the twentieth century began.

In 1900, light-duty soap flakes made their appearance as a more effective means of laundering fine fabrics by hand, and doing diapers and baby clothes in washing machines.

The Era of Detergents

In 1916, a German scientist named Fritz Gunther developed the first synthetic detergent. It was used by industry, but was too harsh for household use. The product was an important breakthrough, however, because scientists had been searching for materials that cleaned like soap but would not leave soap curds on fabrics as soap did. Detergents promised to be the answer.

In 1931, a Procter & Gamble scientist visited laboratories in Germany and Holland and brought back samples of this new product. Could it be refined for consumer use? P&G decided to try.

Two years later, in 1933, Procter & Gamble introduced the first household synthetic detergent, called Dreft. Others followed suit. These early detergents offered an impressive advantage over soap in hard water because they did not form insoluble residues. The one considerable drawback was that, while effective on easily-cleaned surfaces, they did not have the cleaning power to remove difficult stains and soil found in most family washes.

For the next 13 years, scientists searched for a solution. Then, in the early 1940's, complex phosphates were discovered and one of them, sodium tripolyphosphate, proved to be the key to the all-purpose detergents. The first product of this type, P&G's Tide, made its debut in 1946, an event that was to open a new era in product advancement.

Within 10 years, detergents had all but replaced soap as a laundry product. Today, as you read this book, detergent technology has created products to meet every imaginable cleaning need in our homes—dishwashing by hand and automatic dishwasher, surface cleaning and laundering in all its variety.

All this began, if we are to believe the romantic legend—and why not?—at the sacrificial altars on Sapo Hill, a bit of history that well deserves to be remembered.

GLOSSARY OF TERMS

Terms and definitions are taken from "A Handbook of Industry Terms," developed by the Consumer Affairs Committee of The Soap and Detergent Association.

AIR, ROOM, FABRIC FRESHENER/ DEODORIZER

A product intended to counteract the effect of unpleasant odors in the air on certain surfaces and areas in the home.

Such products have been available for many years in liquid, gel and aerosol form. More recently, fragrance-impregnated solids have been introduced in many variations: soft absorbers protected by plastic shielding; plastic or impregnated plastic articles of many shapes; and granular solids in a toilet-roll holder.

The products are available in a variety of fragrances. Some are designed to counteract specific odors, such as those from pets, cooking, or tobacco. Baking soda can be used inside refrigerators and freezers where it absorbs odors arising from food. Borax can also be used as a deodorizer.

Related Terms: Baking Soda, Borax

ABRASIVE

Any of a wide variety of natural or manufactured substances used to smooth, scour, rub away, polish, scrub, etc.

Such naturally occurring mineral abrasives as calcite, feldspar, quartz, pumice and sand are ground to a small particle size and supply scouring and polishing action to cleansers, hand soaps and soap pads. Calcite is lower on the hardness scale and is generally used in those cleansers designed for surfaces, such as Formica® and fiberglass.

Related Terms: Cleanser, Hand Cleanser, Hard Surface Cleaner, Pumice, Silica, Soap Pad

ACID

A chemical substance whose properties include the ability to react with bases or alkalies in water solutions to form salts.

Acids lower the pH of water solutions. When fatty acids, which are organic acids, are reacted with alkalies, soap is produced. Many soils are weakly acidic and are more easily removed in alkaline wash solutions.

Related Terms: Alkali, Fatty Acids, pH, Saponification, Soap

ALKALI

A chemical substance (such as an hydroxide or carbonate of sodium or potassium) which reacts with and neutralizes an acid.

Alkalies are reacted with fats and oils of animal or vegetable origin to form soap. Hard soap is generally made from sodium hydroxide (caustic soda) and soft soap from potassium hydroxide (caustic potash).

Related Terms: Alkalinity, Saponification, Soap

ALKALINITY

A property of water soluble substances (or mixtures) causing the concentration of hydroxyl ions (OH^-) in water solutions to be higher than the concentration of hydrogen ions (H^+).

Alkalinity is exhibited in solution by alkalies such as sodium hydroxide and by alkaline salts such as sodium carbonate.

Soap and soap-based products are alkaline, since soap is a moderately alkaline salt and performs well only in an alkaline medium. Detergent products can be formulated with any desired level of alkalinity as dictated by the needs of the cleaning tasks to be performed. Since the alkalinity is useful in removing acidic, fatty and oily soils, most detergents are more effective on laundry soils when on the alkaline side. Generally, alkalinity is supplied to laundry detergents by builders.

All automatic dishwasher detergents utilize alkalinity, as do most cleansers and hard surface cleaners. In contrast, most hand dishwashing detergents are close to neutrality, performing efficiently without alkalinity because of the mechanical action of hand rubbing with sponge or dishcloth.

Related Terms: Automatic Dishwasher Detergent, Builder, Cleanser, Detergent, Hard Surface Cleaner, pH, Soap, Sodium Carbonate, Surface Active Agent

ALL-PURPOSE CLEANING PRODUCT

A formulation designed for general household cleaning in contrast to specialty cleaning products made to clean in certain situations.

Glossary

Surfaces in a home are made of many materials of different composition and construction. Soils are equally varied and differ in intensity and distribution. No single product can provide optimum performance on all surfaces and soils.

However, there is a range of all-purpose cleaning products, which include nonabrasive products (powders, liquids, sprays) and abrasive all-purpose cleansers, such as scouring powders and liquids and scouring pads.

Related Terms: All-Purpose Detergent, All-Purpose Soap, Cleanser, Hard Surface Cleaner, Soap Pad, Specialty Products

ALL-PURPOSE DETERGENT

A powder or liquid detergent suitable both for laundering and for other household cleaning; now more commonly referred to as heavy duty detergent.

The high sudsing granular products of this detergent type have been widely used for decades, not only in top-loading automatic washers but for hand care of fabrics and for household cleaning tasks ranging from hand dishwashing to floor care. When used for household cleaning, all-purpose detergents may not perform with the same efficiency as products designed for specific purposes. Some all-purpose detergents are not high sudsing.

Related Terms: Built Detergent, Heavy Duty Detergent, Unbuilt Detergent

AMMONIA

An alkaline gas composed of nitrogen and hydrogen (NH_3).

Five-to-ten-percent solutions of ammonia are sold at retail as "household ammonia." A sudsy type that appears somewhat cloudy or milky contains a small amount of soap or detergent.

Household ammonia aids in removing grease and dirt from surfaces such as ovens, tile, windows and mirrors. It is used to some extent as a laundry additive to aid cleaning and is prescribed for treatment of certain stains, like perspiration. Ammonia is included in some hard surface cleaner formulations to assist in grease cutting, wax stripping and general soil removal.

Related Terms: Hard Surface Cleaner

ANIONIC SURFACTANT

A surfactant usually (but not always) derived from an aliphatic hydrocarbon and most commonly in the form of a sodium salt, in which detergency and other properties depend in part on the negatively charged anion of the molecule; hence the name "anionic."

The negative charge (the hydrophilic portion of anionic surfactants carries when in water) can be partially deactivated by interaction with the positively charged water hardness (calcium and magnesium) ions. These surfactants are particularly effective at oily soil cleaning and clay soil suspension, but they need help from other ingredients to reduce the effects of water hardness ions.

The surfactants most widely used in the detergent industry are anionic, and these are usually high sudsing. Linear alkylate sulfonate is the most commonly used anionic surfactant. Others include alkane sulfonate, alkyl ethoxylate sulfate, alkyl glyceryl sulfonate, alkyl sulfate and alpha olefin sulfonate.

Related Terms: Amphoteric Surfactant, Cationic Surfactant, Hydrophilic, Nonionic Surfactant, Surface Active Agent

AUTOMATIC DISHWASHER DETERGENT

A cleaning product designed specifically for use in automatic dishwashers.

It must produce little or no suds or foam because too much foam can inhibit the washing action. Its important functions include the following:

— Tie up water hardness minerals to permit the detergent to do its cleaning job.
— Make water wetter (reduce surface tension) to penetrate and loosen soil.
— Emulsify greasy or oily soil.
— Suppress foam caused by protein soils such as egg and milk.
— Help water to sheet off surfaces, thus minimizing water spots.
— Protect china patterns and metals from the corrosive effects of heat and water alone.

Basic ingredients in most automatic dishwasher detergents include:

Surfactant (nonionic)—lowers the surface tension of water so that it will more quickly wet out the surfaces and the soils, thus allowing water to sheet off dishes and not dry in spots. The surfactant also helps remove and emulsify fatty soils like butter and cooking fat. Nonionic surfactants are used because they generally have the lowest sudsing characteristics.

Glossary

Builder (complex phosphates)—combines with water hardness minerals (primarily calcium and magnesium) and holds them in solution so the minerals cannot combine with food soils and so neither the minerals themselves nor the mineral/food soil combination will leave insoluble spots or film on dishes.

Corrosion inhibitor (sodium silicate)—helps protect dishwasher parts, prevents the removal of china patterns and the corrosion of metals such as aluminum.

Fragrance (optional)—covers the chemical odor of the base product and stale food odors.

Oxidizing agent—helps break down protein soils like egg and milk, aids in removing such stains as coffee or tea and lessens spotting of glassware.

Processing aids—generally inert materials that allow the active ingredients to be combined into a usable form.

Suds suppressor—controls foam from food soils, especially protein soils.

BAKING SODA

The common name for sodium bicarbonate, a mild alkali; it can be helpful in removing acidic soils and can be used for both general and specific cleaning tasks.

The scratchless abrasive action of dry baking soda, when used as a cleanser, helps in removing soil because the undissolved baking soda crystal is harder than soil but softer than sensitive surfaces such as fiberglass. Baking soda can also act as a deodorizer inside refrigerators and freezers where it absorbs odors arising from food.

Related Terms: Acid, Alkali, Sodium Bicarbonate, Specialty Cleaning Product

BATHROOM CLEANER

A category of cleaners including both all-purpose, hard surface cleaning products and specialty types formulated specifically for bathroom cleaning.

The all-purpose products include liquid and powder hard surface cleaners and abrasive household cleansers for scouring difficult stains and soils.

Specialty products include deodorizing and disinfecting cleaners, which usually contain an antimicrobial agent plus a chelating agent to remove hard water scale. They may be in pump spray or aerosol form. Toilet bowl cleaners and in-tank cleaners are specialty products.

Related Terms: Chelating Agent, Cleanser, Disinfectant, Hard Surface Cleaner, Toilet Bowl Cleaner, Tub, Tile, Sink Cleaner

BIODEGRADABILITY

The capability of organic matter to be decomposed by biological processes.

Both the rate and the completeness of decomposition are factors in biodegradability. In the context of detergents, biodegradation refers to decomposition of the organic ingredient in the formulation by bacteria present in waste treatment systems, surface waters, or in the soil. Since surfactants constitute the largest quantity of organic materials in detergent products, their biodegradation is of greatest interest. The surfactants in today's household detergents are readily biodegradable, as is soap.

Related Terms: Surface Active Agent

BLEACH

A product that will clean, whiten, brighten and remove stains from fabrics; it also removes stains on hard surfaces.

Bleach is often used along with a detergent, but unlike a detergent, bleach reacts by the breaking of chemical bonds rather than physical bonds as detergents typically do.

The strongest and most widely used bleach for home laundering is liquid chlorine bleach (usually a sodium hypochlorite solution) which is also capable of disinfecting and deodorizing fabrics. In household cleaning, chlorine bleach is a strong disinfectant and helps eliminate mildew and many other fungi. Dry forms of chlorine bleach are used in automatic dishwasher detergents.

Oxygen bleaches, which are usually powders containing sodium perborate, are used to a lesser degree, but due to their gentler bleaching action, these bleaches can be used on virtually all fabrics and colors. Dry oxygen bleaches are also present in some laundry detergents, additives and presoaks.

Bleaches are typically oxidizing agents; however, reducing bleaches, such as sodium dithionite, have been used in consumer laundry products and are used in industrial and institutional laundry products.

Related Terms: Bleaching, Chlorine Bleach, Color Remover, Laundry Aid, Oxygen Bleach

BLEACHING

A process for removing soils and stains from textile fabrics and hard surfaces by chemical oxidation or reduction.

Related Terms: Bleach

BLUING

A blue coloring material that is added to wash or rinse water and is absorbed on fabrics to counteract the yellowing that sometimes develops in white fabrics after repeated use and laundering.

Bluing produces a blue-white hue on fabrics, which is considered more pleasing to the eye than yellow-white. As a separate laundry additive, bluing may be a blue dye or pigment. It is available: in liquid or dry form for adding to the rinse; in a granular detergent base for adding to washwater along with soap or detergent; and as an ingredient in other laundry products, including detergent, oxygen bleach, fabric softener and starch.

Related Terms: Fluorescent Whitening Agent, Laundry Aid, Ultramarine Blue

BOOSTER

A laundry aid available in granular or liquid form that is formulated to reinforce specific performance characteristics desirable in laundering.

Boosters are designed for use in the wash in addition to the recommended amount of detergent. Liquid boosters can also be used for pretreating stains.

Typical ingredients are: surfactants, builders, borax, enzymes, corrosion inhibitors and fluorescent brighteners. These ingredients are incorporated in widely divergent ratios depending on the objectives of the given product.

Related Terms: Detergent Booster, Laundry Aid

BUILDER

A material that enhances or protects the cleaning efficiency of the surfactant.

Several types of compounds, with different performance capabilities, are used. Builders have a number of functions, principally inactivation of water hardness. This is accomplished either by sequestration (i.e., holding hardness minerals in solution), by precipitation or by ion exchange. Complex phosphates are common sequestering builders. Sodium carbonate is a precipitating builder. Sodium aluminosilicate is an ion exchange builder. Other functions of builders are to supply alkalinity to assist cleaning, especially of acid soils, to provide buffering so alkalinity is maintained at an effective level, to aid in keeping removed soil from redepositing during washing and to emulsify oily and greasy soils.

Related Terms: Alkalinity, Aluminosilicate, Buffer, Built Detergent, Built Soap, NTA, Phosphates, Precipitating Agent, Sequestering Agent, Sodium Carbonate, Sodium Citrate, Sodium Silicate, Sodium Tripolyphosphate, Surface Active Agent, Tetrapotassium Pyrophosphate, Tetrasodium Pyrophosphate, Trisodium Phosphate

BUILT DETERGENT

A cleaning product containing both surfactant and builder.

Home laundering makes use of built detergents because of their effective performance on specific soils (clay and body). Ingredients used in formulations along with surfactant and builder include fluorescent whitening agent, antiredeposition agent, corrosion inhibitor, suds control agent, oxygen bleach, colorant, fragrance, enzyme, bluing and processing aids. Not all of these ingredients are used in every built detergent. Inclusion of antiredeposition and whitening agents, corrosion inhibitor, colorant, fragrance and processing aids is customary.

Complex phosphates (especially sodium tripolyphosphate), sodium carbonate and sodium silicate are the builders most commonly used. (Sodium silicate is also a corrosion inhibitor.) Borax, sodium citrate and soap are used to a lesser extent.

Built detergents may be granular or liquid in form and produce high, medium, or low suds. Since built detergents are designed for doing laundry, they are classified as laundry detergents. They are also considered heavy duty. Those that are high sudsing are adapted to many non-laundry household cleaning tasks and are termed "all-purpose."

Related Terms: All-Purpose Detergent, Builder, Heavy Duty Detergent, Laundry Detergent

CATIONIC SURFACTANT

A surfactant with a positively charged ionic group.

The most commonly used cationic surfactants are known as quaternary ammonium compounds, such as alkyl dimethyl benzyl ammonium chloride. Some are widely used in disinfecting/sanitizing household and bathroom cleaners. Others are active ingredients in wash/rinse/dryer fabric softeners. Alone they are not effective cleaners but may be part of a complex surfactant system.

Related Terms: Amine Oxide, Amphoteric Surfactant, Anionic Surfactant, Disinfectant, Fabric Softener, Nonionic Surfactant, Quaternary Ammonium Compounds

Glossary

CHLORINE BLEACH   A group of strong oxidizing agents, all of which have one or more chlorine atoms in their molecule.

Liquid chlorine bleach is commonly sold as an approximately 5% solution of sodium hypochlorite. As a laundry additive, liquid chlorine bleach removes stains, aids in soil removal, whitens, disinfects and deodorizes. Dry forms of chlorine bleach include chlorinated isocyanurates and chlorinated trisodium phosphate. They are used as the bleaching ingredient in products marketed in dry form, such as cleansers and automatic dishwasher detergents. Neither liquid nor dry chlorine bleach should be used on silks, woolens, dyes sensitive to hypochlorite and certain stains, such as rust, which can be set by hypochlorite. Chlorine bleach deactivates enzymes found in laundry detergents or laundry aids.

Related Terms: Bleach, Chlorinated Isocyanurate, Chlorinated Trisodium Phosphate, Hypochlorite, Oxygen Bleach, Perborate

CLEANSER   A powdered cleaning product usually containing an abrasive, a surfactant and sometimes a bleach.

The abrasive is usually calcium carbonate (soft), feldspar (moderately hard), or silica (hard). Softer materials are usually preferred in products for surfaces such as Formica® and fiberglass. The abrasive supplies scouring and polishing action. The surfactant aids in cleaning and in suspension and emulsification of removed soil. Bleach may be chlorinated trisodium phosphate or chlorinated isocyanurate. It aids in stain and soil removal, deodorizes and disinfects. Colorant, fragrance, alkalies and builders such as sodium tripolyphosphate and tetrasodium pyrophosphate are also commonly used in cleanser formulations.

Liquid cleansers, in which the abrasive is suspended in a surfactant solution or thickening agent, are also available. Liquid cleansers are generally made with abrasives, such as calcium carbonate or pearlite, but harder materials such as silica can also be used. Fragrance is a common ingredient in liquid cleansers. Optional ingredients include bleach and other detergent components.

Related Terms: Abrasive, Chlorinated Isocyanurate, Chlorinated Trisodium Phosphate, Scouring Powder, Surface Active Agent

CORROSION INHIBITOR   A material that protects against the wearing away of appliance surfaces.

Sodium silicate is the corrosion inhibitor used in detergents and built soap. It is incorporated in laundry and automatic dishwasher products to protect washer and dishwasher metal parts and finishes, especially porcelain enamel. In an automatic dishwasher detergent, sodium silicate also protects china and metal utensils.

Related Terms: Automatic Dishwasher Detergent, Laundry Detergent, Sodium Silicate

DETERGENCY

The ability to clean or remove soil.

Generally detergency is associated with the action of a cleaning agent such as soap, detergent, alkaline salt, or a combination of these. In the context of consumer cleaning products, especially those designed for washing clothes and dishes, detergency can be described as the removal of soil by employing one or more of the following mechanisms (generally in conjunction with mechanical action):

1. Lowering surface and interfacial tensions
2. Solubilization of soils
3. Emulsification of soils
4. Suspension/dispersion of removed soils
5. Saponification of fatty soils and enzymatic digestion of protein-based soils
6. Inactivation of water hardness
7. Neutralization of acid soils

Related Terms: Alkalinity, Detergent, Emulsification, Sequestering Agent, Soap, Surface Active Agent, Water Softener

DETERGENT

Technically, any cleansing agent. In popular usage, washing and cleaning agents with a composition other than soap that clean by much the same mechanisms as does soap.

The term detergent is used to describe both the basic surface active agents and finished products. The finished products are synthesized chemically from a variety of raw materials derived from petroleum, fatty acids and other sources. They may also contain ingredients such as builders, antiredeposition agents, corrosion inhibitors, suds control agents, enzymes, fabric softeners, fluorescent whitening agents, sodium sulfate, water, alcohols, hydrotropes, colorants, fragrances and opacifiers.

Detergent ingredients vary with the types of products, which include light duty detergents, heavy duty detergents, hard surface cleaners, automatic dishwasher detergents and cleansers. The finished product comes in a number of forms, such as granules, liquids and crystals.

Related Terms: All-Purpose Cleaning Product, All-Purpose Detergent, Built Detergent, Heavy Duty Detergent, Laundry Detergent, Light Duty Detergent, Unbuilt Detergent

DISINFECTANT

An agent that frees from infection by destroying harmful bacteria but not necessarily all bacterial spores.

In relation to home laundering, washing with a soap or detergent in a modern washer, using recommended laundering procedures followed by drying, provides hygienically acceptable domestic laundry under normal circumstances. When special efforts are desirable or needed (for example, when there is infectious illness), disinfectants for use in laundering are available. The most common is liquid chlorine bleach, but it cannot be used on all fabrics. For nonbleachable loads, there are three other types of disinfectants:

— Quaternary Ammonium Compounds - effective only if the "active" ingredient is sufficiently high in activity and concentration; should be used only in the rinse since they may be deactivated by soap and detergent.
— Phenolic Compounds - also depend on a sufficiently high active content; can be used in wash or rinse water.
— Pine Oil Products - effective when they contain at least 70% pine oil; may be added to wash or rinse. Disinfectant products containing lower concentrations of pine oil include additional active ingredients.

Hard surfaces can be disinfected by hard surface cleaners having disinfecting properties as stated on the label and by cleansers containing chlorine bleaching agents in dry form.

Products making disinfectant claims must be registered with the U.S. Environmental Protection Agency, and it will be stated on the label.

Related Terms: Antimicrobial, Bactericide, Germicide, Laundry Aid

ENZYMES

A large class of complex proteinaceous molecules, which act as catalysts in biochemical reactions.

Selected types of enzymes are useful in laundering, where

they break down certain soils and stains to simpler forms, which are then more readily and completely removed by the laundry soap or detergent. To function most effectively on stubborn soils and stains, enzymes should be used with either high concentration such as direct application in pretreatment of soils, or extended exposure such as in presoaking, longer than the usual wash period of 10-15 minutes. Enzymes' effectiveness is deactivated by liquid chlorine bleach, so the two must be used separately to obtain the full benefit of each. Enzymes are used in laundry detergent liquids, powders and boosters.

Related Terms: Amylase, Presoak Products, Protease

ETCHING

A chemical change in the surface of glassware.

Incipient etching can be recognized by iridescent coloration of the glass. As etching progresses this changes the opaqueness, which appears similar to filming except that it cannot be removed. Etching is primarily associated with automatic dishwashing, less often with hand washing. Soft water, high water temperatures (above 140°F) and high pH intensify it. Mechanical etching can occur when two glasses rub against each other in the dishwasher.

Related Terms: Filming

EUTROPHICATION

A term derived from Greek words meaning "to nourish well" and referring to increased levels of nutrients in a lake or other body of water.

Lakes age naturally, becoming filled with plants and silt, forming marshes and finally, solid land. This aging process (from a young or oligotrophic state to a mature or eutrophic state) normally takes thousands of years, but man's activities can greatly speed up the process by increasing the supply of nutrients entering the lake. These nutrients include phosphorus, nitrogen, carbon, potassium, trace elements and vitamins. Sources include human, animal and industrial wastes, agricultural and urban runoff, soil erosion and even a sizable amount transported by the air.

Increases in nutrients cause rising rates of productivity, chiefly in the form of explosive growths or "blooms" of algae. Decay of this algae can result in decreased oxygen levels in the deeper, colder layers of large lakes, killing fish. Steps which can be taken to reverse the eutrophication process involve reducing the level of nutrients entering water bodies through treatment of wastewater and reduction of runoff. Some areas also ban phosphate laundry detergents, although the fraction of phosphate they contribute to most lakes and streams is small.

Related Terms: Detergent, Phosphates

FABRIC SOFTENER

A laundry additive that gives fabrics a soft feel and smooth surface, reduces static electricity and wrinkling and makes ironing easier.

Most fabric softeners are designed for addition to the rinse or drying cycles, but a few are available for the wash. Wash and rinse added types are liquids; dryer-added fabric softeners come as sprays, impregnated tear-off sheets and impregnated foam (porous) sheets, or as a slow dispensing solid bar that attaches to the fin of a dryer. The softening agents most commonly used are cationic quaternary ammonium compounds. Bluing is frequently included, as well as fragrance. Infrequently, antimicrobial ingredients or fluorescent whitening agents are added.

Fabric softening ingredients also are incorporated in some laundry detergent products.

Related Terms: Laundry Aids, Quaternary Ammonium Compounds

FILMING

The development of a thin covering or coating.

In automatic dishwashing, filming usually refers to a deposit of mineral salts. It generally occurs when the water is high in hardness salts or total solids and is most noticeable on clear glassware. Filming can also be a result of incompletely removed soil, especially protein or fat residues. The result may range from a thin transparent film to an opaque coating, and can usually be removed by increasing the amount of detergent or by using a vinegar rinse. These approaches will not work if a surface is opaque because of etching.

Related Terms: Etching

FLUORESCENT WHITENING AGENT (FWA)

A chemical compound that creates a visual whitening or brightening effect when exposed to near ultraviolet radiation by virtue of fluorescence, i.e., the conversion of invisible ultraviolet light into visible blue light.

The fluorescent whitening agents used by the detergent industry share the further characteristic of adsorbing to fabrics during household laundering. The whiteness or brightness of the laundry is thus enhanced. FWA is included in all-purpose soap and detergent and some light duty and laundry aid products. Its effectiveness varies with type of fabric and concentration in the washwater, which is always very low. Its effect is cumulative to a degree, so new fabrics exhibit increased fluorescence over a period of washes. Eventually, however, a leveling-off point is reached.

In recent years an increasing number of fabrics have been prebrightened in manufacture, i.e., have incorporated FWAs, especially the acrylic and polyester fabrics.

Related Terms: Bluing, Brightener, Optical Brightener

GERMICIDE

Any material that kills germs.

The term germicide is essentially synonymous with bactericide, but it may be somewhat broader in the range of its coverage and somewhat less precise. Most soap or detergent products that contain a germicide make sanitizing/disinfecting claims.

Related Terms: Antimicrobial, Bactericide, Disinfectant

GRANULES

Small particles or grains, as in granulated sugar, either hollow blown or ordinary powders.

An important industry development was the adaptation of the spray-drying process to soap and detergent manufacturing, which provided the means of producing high quality granular finished products, which dissolve readily in use. In spray drying, hot liquid soap or detergent is pumped into a tall tower, where it is sprayed as a fine mist. As the mist falls it is dried by hot air and falls to the bottom as granules. Particle size, degree of puffing and density of finished product can be varied by changing conditions of operation.

Related Terms: Flakes, Powder

HARD SURFACE CLEANER

A product formulated for cleaning painted surfaces, washable floor coverings, plastics, metals, porcelain and other surfaces.

Glossary

Hard surface cleaners come in a variety of physical forms and formulas. There are powders that must be dissolved before use, liquids that can be diluted or used full strength and liquids with mechanical pump dispensers or in aerosol containers. The powders generally depend on builders to enhance cleaning and reduce filming and streaking. The liquid detergent formulations are highly individualized. They all have a soap or detergent surfactant base and, generally, water-softening ingredients (such as EDTA and potassium pyrophosphate) and alkaline builders, such as sodium carbonate. Petroleum distillates and pine oil may be included for grease and oil cutting. Those products designed to deodorize/disinfect as well as clean normally contain pine oil, quaternary ammonia, or phenol disinfectants.

Related Terms: Alkalinity, Disinfectant

HARD WATER (See Water Hardness)

HEAVY DUTY DETERGENT OR SOAP A term that describes products designed for doing the total family laundry, including heavily soiled items. They may usually be used for general household cleaning tasks as well.

Related Terms: All-Purpose Detergent, All-Purpose Soap, Built Detergent, Built Soap, Laundry Detergent

HOUSEHOLD CLEANER (See Hard Surface Cleaner)

HYDROPHILIC Water loving: defined by the American Society for Testing and Materials as "a descriptive term applied to the group or radical of a surfactant molecule that makes or tends to make it soluble in water."

Associated with the hydrophilic portion of a surfactant molecule is the opposite hydrophobic (water hating) portion. The special capabilities of surfactants in loosening dirt are a direct consequence of these incompatible component parts, which have opposite attractions toward dirt and toward water.

Related Terms: Surface Active Agent

HYDROPHOBIC (See Hydrophilic)

LAUNDRY AID

A product that contributes to the effectiveness of laundry detergents and/or provides specialized performance.

Related Terms: Bleach, Bluing, Color Remover, Detergent Booster, Disinfectant, Fabric Softener, Pretreat Soil and Stain Remover, Presoak Product, Starch, Sizing, Washing Soda, Water Softener

LAUNDRY DETERGENT

A product containing a surfactant and other ingredients, formulated to clean and care for the many different fabrics in the family wash.

Next to the surfactant, a builder is an important ingredient in formulated laundry detergents. Builders have a number of functions, principally inactivation of water hardness, which interferes with good cleaning. Built detergent types include granules and liquids. Some liquid detergents are unbuilt, containing surfactants that are relatively insensitive to water hardness.

Other customary ingredients of laundry detergents include antiredeposition agents, corrosion inhibitors, fluorescent whitening agents, colorants, fragrance and processing aids. Optional ingredients include suds control agents, bleach, borax, enzymes, bluing, fabric softener and soil release agent.

Some laundry detergents are denser or more concentrated than others. Density or concentration influences the amount of product recommended for the wash. Detergents also vary in sudsing characteristics, ranging from high to low suds levels. Different suds levels are provided for reasons of compatibility with washer design and to satisfy consumer preferences.

Depending on the presence of other ingredients in the laundry detergent formulation, some products offer special benefits in addition to the expected cleaning. Thus, certain laundry detergents are especially effective at lower washing temperatures; others provide additional fabric care benefits, such as softening, static control and wrinkle reduction.

Related Terms: All-Purpose Detergent, Built Detergent

LAUNDRY SOAP BAR

Heavy duty or built soap in bar form.

The fat base of a laundry soap bar is usually tallow, with rosin added for quicker solubility. Borax and builders, such as sodium silicate and sodium carbonate, are added to improve performance and help soften hard water. Laundry soap bars were first displaced by more convenient chip and granule forms. Today, these have been largely supplanted by laundry detergents. Laundry soap bars are used for pretreating heavily soiled and stained items before machine washing or for hand washing hosiery or lingerie.

Related Terms: Heavy Duty Soap, Soap, Tallow Soap

LIGHT DUTY DETERGENT

An unbuilt, or infrequently low-level-built, detergent-based washing product designed for light cleaning tasks, especially hand dishwashing.

While not made for general laundering, it does find use in hand washing lightly soiled, delicate garments and in household cleaning tasks where ability to handle heavy soil is not required.

Originally introduced as granules, today's light duty detergents are usually liquids. Emphasis in formulation is on hand dishwashing, which places a premium on a product's ability to handle all food soils, its mildness to hands, plentiful long-lasting suds and rinsing that leaves surfaces free of film and spots. Light duty detergents are based principally on anionic surfactants, which are generally high sudsing, but they may also contain some nonionic surfactants. Other commonly used ingredients are ethyl alcohol, suds boosters and stabilizers such as acyl or fatty acid ethanolamides, opacifying and/or colorant agents and fragrance.

Related Terms: Amine Oxide, Unbuilt Detergent

LIGHT DUTY SOAP

A soap containing little or no builder, designed for the care of baby clothes and fine fabrics, and hand dishwashing.

Light duty soaps may contain FWA and fragrance and can be made in flake, granular and bar form.

Related Terms: Unbuilt Soap

LIME SOAP

The insoluble salt formed by the interaction of soaps and fatty acids with the minerals in hard water; it is commonly referred to as soap curd.

The use of the word lime in this term may come from the fact that limestone areas generally foster hard water, or from the fact that the words lime and calcium are closely associated. Calcium and magnesium fatty acid salts are very insoluble and precipitate immediately on formation. Since they tend to agglomerate (cluster together), they form curd-like masses. They also tend to adhere to surfaces, thus causing filming or deposits, such as bathtub ring.

The problems lime soap causes spurred the development of mechanical water softeners, packaged water softeners and the technology leading to new surfactants and builders and detergent products based on them.

Related Terms: Soap Curd, Water Conditioner, Water Hardness, Water Softener

LIQUID CHLORINE BLEACH

A solution of sodium hypochlorite, a highly active oxidizing agent.

Liquid chlorine bleach is also called household bleach or simply liquid bleach and is commonly distributed as an approximately 5% solution of sodium hypochlorite.

Related Terms: Bleach, Chlorine Bleach, Hypochlorite

LIQUID DETERGENT

Liquid detergents may be formulated as heavy duty laundry detergents, light duty detergents, or hard surface cleaners.

Heavy duty liquid laundry detergents are manufactured with or without a builder. Liquid detergents that do not contain a builder generally contain a high percentage of surfactant. Some of these detergents contain nonionic surfactants and some contain a combination of anionic and nonionic surfactants. Currently the builders in liquid products are sodium citrate and soap (fatty acid salts). Other ingredients include fluorescent whitening agents, possibly a corrosion inhibitor, an antiredeposition agent, enzymes, fabric softener and fragrance.

Light duty liquid products are used for laundering lightly soiled items or for hand dishwashing. They are not suitable for machine washing because of their high sudsing characteristics. The surfactant, which is their most important ingredient, is often a mixed anionic/nonionic system. Most of the products do not contain a builder.

Liquid hard surface cleaners use a moderate amount of surfactant, generally both anionic and nonionic. Solvent materials such as various alcohols, pine oil, or naphtha are used to handle oily or greasy soils. Builders are used at moderate or low level depending on the product. Some of the products may contain a disinfectant.

Related Terms: Alcohol, Alcohol Ethoxylate, Alkyl Glyceryl Sulfonate, Built Detergent, Detergent, Hard Surface Cleaner, Laundry

Detergent, Light Duty Detergent, Opacifier, Pretreat Soil and Stain Remover, Sodium Citrate, Surface Active Agent, Unbuilt Detergent

NONIONIC SURFACTANT

A surface active agent that contains neither positively nor negatively charged (ionic) functional groups; such surfactants have been found to be particularly effective in removing oily soil.

In contrast to anionic and cationic surfactants, nonionic surfactants do not ionize in solution. Some nonionics are low sudsing and are found in low sudsing laundry detergents, pretreat stain removers, hard surface cleaners and machine dishwashing detergents. Commonly used types include ethoxylated alcohols and alkyl amine oxides.

Related Terms: Anionic Surfactant, Cationic Surfactant, Surface Active Agent

OXYGEN BLEACH

A laundry product containing inorganic peroxygen compounds, which release active oxygen in wash water. This type of product produces gentler bleaching (oxidizing) action than chlorine bleach.

The most frequently used oxygen bleach is sodium perborate (usually referred to simply as perborate), with potassium monopersulfate, sodium percarbonate and hydrogen peroxide used less frequently. Oxygen bleach can be used safely on most fabrics, colors and fabric finishes, including those where the use of chlorine bleach is not recommended.

Perborate is available in dry laundry bleach and is also an ingredient in laundry detergent, presoak products and cleanser. A solution of hydrogen peroxide is marketed as a liquid oxygen bleach.

Powdered oxygen bleaches also contain a builder, usually sodium carbonate, which provides additional alkalinity and allows the perborate to function more effectively as a bleach. Other ingredients such as surfactants, enzymes, brighteners, bluing agents and fragrance can be incorporated into both liquid and powdered formulations.

Related Terms: Bleach, Chlorine Bleach, Perborate

PHOSPHATES

Salts of the various phosphoric acids.

The complex phosphates are a group of sequestering agents widely used in detergent formulations (except where phosphates are banned by law) because of their superiority in water softening, sequestering and other builder functions. Sodium tripolyphosphate was the original builder upon which modern laundry detergent technology developed and is used in laundry granules, automatic dishwasher detergents and cleansers. It is adaptable to the spray drying process by which granules are made. Tetrasodium pyrophosphate is also used in detergent granules, but since it does not rank as high in over-all performance as sodium tripolyphosphate, its application is more limited. Highly soluble tetrapotassium pyrophosphate is used in hard surface cleaners and industrial and institutional cleaners, where it serves as a builder, water softener and source of alkalinity.

Another complex phosphate, sodium metaphosphate, is marketed as a packaged water softener. The most widely used sodium metaphosphate is sodium hexametaphosphate (SHMP), which softens by sequestering.

The orthophosphate form of phosphates, trisodium phosphate (also called sodium orthophosphate), is a water softener that inactivates hardness minerals by precipitation. It is used primarily in powdered cleansers as a source of alkalinity and for its water-softening properties.

Related Terms: Alkalinity, Builder, Precipitating Agent, Sequestering Agent, Water Softener

PINE OIL

The oil obtained by steam distillation and subsequent processing of gum taken from pine trees, or recovered as a by-product of paper pulp-making by the sulfate process.

Pine oil's principal application in household cleaning is in liquid hard surface cleaners, where it is a popular ingredient because of its characteristic aroma and its sanitizing/disinfecting properties.

Related Terms: Disinfectant, Fragrance Materials, Hard Surface Cleaner, Pine Oil Cleaner

PINE OIL CLEANER

A liquid hard surface cleaner, characterized by a soap or detergent base and pine oil among the major ingredients.

The pine oil provides solvent action for oil and fatty soils, paints and tars; sanitizing/disinfecting properties; and fragrance. The soap or detergent supplies the basic cleaning power.

Related Terms: Hard Surface Cleaner, Pine Oil

PRESOAK

A soaking operation that precedes the regular laundering process.

Presoaking is generally employed for laundry that presents unusual problems in regard to stains or soil level, or when extra cleaning action is considered advisable, e.g., for diapers and baby clothes. Soak water should be warm or cool depending on the type of stain. Length of soaking is determined by the job to be done; usually a minimum of thirty minutes is needed to produce major benefits. Prolonged soaking (more than overnight) is not recommended.

Some automatic washers provide presoak cycles, with a brief period of agitation, a soak period and a spin out. The exact nature of the cycle varies with make and model. For automatic washers that do not provide a presoak cycle, the dial can be manipulated by hand. Whatever the means employed, presoaking should be followed by wringing or spinning (or at least by emptying the soak water) and then by a regular wash with laundry soap or detergent.

Related Terms: Presoak Products

PRESOAK PRODUCTS

Products designed primarily for soaking stained or heavily soiled articles prior to regular laundering; they are also used in the washwater along with detergent.

The special contribution of a major group of presoak products is the stain removal and soil loosening action of their enzymes. Two enzyme types, amylase and protease, are used on a broad spectrum of stains. Also included to augment the enzyme action are builders and surfactants, plus optional ingredients such as fragrance, bluing, colorant and sodium perborate. Builder ingredients may include sodium tripolyphosphate, if permitted by law, and frequently sodium silicate and sodium carbonate. Less frequently used, mostly in non-phosphate formulations, are sodium bicarbonate and sodium citrate.

Enzymes require time to do their work. When a half hour, or more for very difficult tasks, can be allotted, the presoak operation makes full use of enzymatic activity. Enzymes are deactivated by chlorine bleach, so enzyme presoaks and chlorine bleach should not be used together.

Another presoak group, used for diaper soaking, usually contains enzymes and has borax as a basic ingredient.

Related Terms: Amylase, Borax, Diaper Soaking Product, Enzymes, Prewash, Protease

PRETREATMENT

Procedures that may be used prior to laundering or dishwashing to handle special or unusual problems, such as spots, stains, or heavy soil that are unlikely to be removed by washing alone.

Laundry pretreatment procedures in common use include:
— Soaking (presoaking) - Especially helpful for general problems of heavy soil and stains. Special presoak products are useful for treating generalized staining, while regular laundry detergent is helpful in cases of heavy soil.
— Direct Application (for soil lines) - Soil lines, as on shirt collars, and small stained areas can be pretreated by dampening the soiled area and rubbing in a paste of detergent granules, bar soap, liquid detergent, or laundry additive.
— Special Treatment (for difficult stains) - The precise method and product for removing difficult stains vary with the kind of stain. Stain-removal charts are widely available. Also available are soil and stain removers, special laundry products that come in aerosol, liquid and solid stick form. The products containing solvent are useful for treating oily and greasy stains, for which permanent press and synthetic fiber fabrics have an affinity.

In dishwashing, pretreatment usually refers to anything done prior to the normal washing process. This includes scraping, rinsing and soaking.

Related Terms: Pretreat Soil and Stain Removers, Presoak Products, Spotting

PREWASH

A short wash preceding the regular machine wash cycle, usually employed for loads with heavy particulate soil or when special cleaning is desired as in washing diapers.

Regular laundry detergent should be used in the prewash and in the full wash period that follows. Some automatic washers provide a prewash cycle followed by spinning to extract the soiled water.

Related Terms: Presoak

Glossary

RINSE AGENT

A nonionic surfactant or wetting agent which, when injected into the last rinse of a dishwasher cycle, lowers surface tension, thus improving draining of the water from the dishes and utensils.

Dishwasher rinse agents come in both a solid bar and liquid form, the liquid for use in dishwashers equipped with a rinse aid dispenser, the bar for machines without a dispenser. By improving draining of the last rinse, spotting and filming, caused by water solids that remain after drying, are minimized.

Related Terms: Water Hardness

RUST REMOVER

A product that removes rust stains from fabrics, dishwashers and other washable surfaces, such as bathrooms, kitchens, tea kettles, dishes and glassware and wherever water comes in contact.

Most commonly, these materials are composed of reducing agents (such as sodium hydrosulfite) or acid products and may be in liquid, powder, or gel form. During laundering, some rust removers may be used in the regular laundry cycle or for presoaking. They may also be useful for miscellaneous stain removal, such as removal of dyebleeding.

Rust removers made to remove rust, scale and lime deposits from the inside of dishwashers are a combination of acids. Used periodically as needed, they are added at the beginning of the main wash cycle (no dishes or other cleanser present) and are allowed to remain through the balance of the cycles.

Related Terms: Color Remover, Stripping Agent

SANITIZER

An agent that reduces the number of bacterial contaminants to safe levels as determined by public health requirements.

The term sanitizing generally refers to inanimate objects (particularly food-related utensils, equipment surfaces) and implies providing a satisfactory condition of cleanliness in addition to a safe bacterial level. Thus, detergent sanitizers combine cleaning and sanitizing. The same kinds of compounds that provide disinfecting action in cleansers and hard surface cleaners also contribute sanitizing capability.

Related Terms: Disinfectant, Hard Surface Cleaner

SAPONIFICATION

The process of converting a fat into soap by treating it with an alkali.

This may be done by boiling fat and alkali in a kettle under controlled conditions. They react to form soap and glycerin. Modern methods make soap in continuous processes either by treating fat with alkali or by first splitting the fat into fatty acids and glycerin by a process called hydrolysis. The fatty acids are purified by distillation and then mixed with the correct amount of alkali to convert them into soap.

Related Terms: Fatty Acids, Glycerin, Soap

SEQUESTERING AGENT

"Any compound that, in aqueous solution, combines with a metallic ion to form a water-soluble combination in which the ion is substantially inactive." (American Society for Testing and Materials definition)

Complex phosphates are sequestrants, since they have the ability to inactivate the water hardness metals (calcium and magnesium) and iron and manganese without precipitation. Water softening without precipitation, i.e., by sequestration, distinguishes the complex phosphates from compounds such as sodium carbonate and sodium orthophosphate, which soften by precipitation of the hardness metals.

Related Terms: Chelating Agent, Phosphates, Precipitating Agent, Sodium Citrate, Water Softener

SOAP

"The product formed by the saponification or neutralization of fats, oils, waxes, rosins, or their acids with organic or inorganic bases." (American Society for Testing and Materials definition)

This definition of soap covers a wide range of compositions, but in the area of consumer products, soap usually means the sodium or potassium salt of animal fat or a combination of vegetable oil and animal fat. The principal fats and oils used are tallow and coconut oil. In common usage, the word soap is also employed generically to describe any washing product that is preponderantly soap or depends on soap for its primary function. Thus toilet and laundry bars, light duty flakes and granules and all-purpose built products are all termed soap, if soap is their base ingredient.

Glossary

Soap performs its principal task, cleaning, by various mechanisms, including reducing surface tension (it is an anionic surfactant), loosening, dispersing and suspending particulate soil, emulsifying fatty and oily matter and providing alkalinity. Soaps are mildly alkaline. The major drawback to soap, particularly in laundering, is that it forms insoluble lime soap (soap curd) with water hardness minerals, which is deposited on fabrics and in washing machines. It was this problem that spurred the development of detergents, which are relatively unaffected by hard water and as a result have largely replaced soap for laundry purposes.

Related Terms: All-Purpose Soap, Built Soap, Light Duty Soap, Saponification, Surface Active Agent, Toilet Soap

SOAP CURD

The insoluble precipitate that forms when soap is used in hard water. Soap curd and lime soap are synonymous.

Related Terms: Lime Soap, Water Hardness

SODIUM CARBONATE

A fairly strong alkaline salt occurring naturally as soda ash.

Sodium carbonate finds wide use as a builder in laundry detergents and as a source of alkalinity in powdered hard surface cleaners and presoak products. Sodium carbonate supplies alkaline cleaning power and also softens water by precipitating the hardness minerals out of solution. It is also called soda ash and is available on the retail market in a hydrated crystalline form under the name "washing soda."

Related Terms: Builder, Washing Soda, Water Softener

SODIUM CITRATE

The sodium salt of citric acid.

Sodium citrate sequesters hardness minerals and is used as a builder in some non-phosphate products. Its principal application is in liquid laundry detergents; it also is used in some presoak products.

Related Terms: Builder, Citrate, Citric Acid, Sequestering Agent, Water Hardness, Water Softener

SODIUM SILICATE

A sodium salt of silicic acid.

Related Terms: Silicate

The How To Clean Handbook

SODIUM SULFATE

The sodium salt of sulfuric acid.

Sodium sulfate is present in most granular detergents, both as a result of its formation during processing of the surfactant and, in some cases, because of the inclusion of additional amounts. Sodium sulfate improves the physical state of detergent granules by aiding pourability and by making the granules crisper. It also provides a means of adjusting density so the finished product supplies the desired amount of surfactant, builders and other active ingredients per unit of volume (such as a cup). Sodium sulfate is essentially a neutral compound, neither alkaline nor acidic. It is considered both a processing or manufacturing aid and a quality control agent.

Related Terms: Formula Stabilizing Agent, Quality Control Agent

SPOTTING

The process of specially treating isolated spots and stains that are not likely to come out in the normal washing process.

Spotting is a form of pretreatment oriented toward problems requiring specialized individual attention rather than toward general problems, such as grass staining or heavy soil, where soaking is more practical. Stain removal charts provide information on treatment procedures. Rubbing in soap or detergent prior to laundering is effective in removing difficult soil, such as soil lines on shirt collars and cuffs.

Related Terms: Pretreatment

STAIN

A visible discoloration.

A stain may be one or more relatively small spots or a fairly large area of discoloration. Instructions are available from many sources for removing stains from washable fabrics. Among techniques are presoaking and other pretreatment, bleaching and special use of detergent or of special materials appropriate to the particular stain.

Related Terms: Bleach, Presoak, Pretreatment, Prewash, Spotting

STARCH

Chemically, starch refers to complex carbohydrates obtained from vegetable sources.

Glossary

In home laundry usage, the term has been expanded to cover products that perform the same function as starch, i.e., supplying body or stiffness to fabrics, but that are based on synthesized chemicals such as carboxymethylcellulose or polyvinyl acetate. The latter are called synthetic or plastic starches.

Vegetable starch comes as: 1) dry, uncooked starch (lump, cube, or powder) which must be mixed with hot water or cooked before use; 2) pre-cooked flakes which can be mixed with cold water; 3) a concentrated pre-cooked solution; 4) a concentrated solution in an aerosol container for spraying directly on fabrics while ironing. Synthetic or plastic starches come as liquids and in aerosol form for direct application. The liquids are available in soluble form which is removed in the next laundering. More durable varieties last through several washes.

Besides supplying body and stiffness, starch gives ironed articles a fresh smooth appearance, helps garments stay clean longer because of the harder, smoother surface and facilitates soil removal in the next wash since the soil becomes imbedded in the starch, not the fabric.

Related Terms: Laundry Aid, Sizing

SUDS

A mass of bubbles formed on the surface of a liquid by agitation.

Most soap products suds fairly readily and voluminously, provided there is sufficient agitation and an excess of soap over that required to overcome the hardness of the water. Detergents vary widely in sudsing properties.

The words "suds" and "foam" are interchangeable. In home laundering, suds also refers to the washwater or to the washing segment of the laundry cycle.

Related Terms: Foam, Lather, Sudsing

SURFACE ACTIVE AGENT

An organic chemical that, when added to a liquid, changes the properties of that liquid at a surface.

This is a basic function for products serving as detergents and as wetting, foaming, dispersing, emulsifying and penetrating agents. Surface active agent is commonly shortened to surfactant.

Surfactants are classified by whether or not they ionize in solution and by the nature of their ionic or electrical charges. Categories of charges are called anionic, nonionic, cationic, or amphoteric. The anionic and nonionic surfactant types (for example, LAS, ethoxylated alcohol, alkyl sulfate, alpha olefin sulfonate and soap) possess good cleaning properties and are important ingredients in household soaps and detergents.

In most detergent products designed for washing clothes and dishes, the surfactant is a basic ingredient; soap is basic to most body-washing products. All surfactants and soaps perform the important function of lowering water's surface tension, commonly known as making water "wetter." This enables the cleaning solution more quickly to wet out the surface being cleaned so soil can be readily loosened and removed (usually with the aid of mechanical action). Surfactants are also instrumental in removing soils, both fatty and particulate, and in keeping them emulsified, suspended and dispersed so that settling back on the surface is minimized.

In addition to their leading role in laundry and light duty formulations, surfactants are used to some degree in most other household cleaning and washing products. They are the base of most liquid hard surface cleaners. Relatively small amounts of surfactant are usually included in powdered hard surface cleaners, cleansers and automatic dishwasher detergents. Specialized surfactant applications include the use of cationics (quaternary ammonium compounds) to provide deodorizing and disinfecting action, while nonionic wetting agents are available for adding to the last rinse in automatic dishwashing to provide better draining of rinse water.

Related Terms: Amphoteric Surfactant, Anionic Surfactant, Automatic Dishwasher Detergent, Bathroom Cleaner, Built Detergent, Cationic Surfactant, Hard Surface Cleaner, Laundry Detergent, Light Duty Detergent, Nonionic Surfactant, Quaternary Ammonium Compounds, Rinse Agent

SYNTHETIC DETERGENT

A term describing washing and cleaning products based on synthetic surfactants rather than traditional soaps.

Over a period of years the adjective "synthetic" (which in this context means put together chemically, or synthesized from a variety of raw materials) has been gradually dropped so that today

Glossary

non-soap washing and cleaning products are simply called detergents.

Related Terms: All-Purpose Cleaning Product, All-Purpose Detergent, Built Detergent, Heavy Duty Detergent, Laundry Detergent, Light Duty Detergent, Unbuilt Detergent

TOILET BOWL CLEANER

A specialty cleaning product.

Toilet bowl cleaners are designed to maintain a clean and pleasant smelling bowl and some also disinfect. Their many different forms include thickened liquids that cling to the sides of the bowl, fresheners that keep the bowl smelling fresh and various forms of in-tank cleaners that release active ingredients into the bowl with each flush.

Surfactants are the primary ingredient for soil removal. Some cleaners contain acids or sequestrants to facilitate removal of stains caused by hard water deposits. Specific organic stains are also cleaned by bleaching agents provided by some products.

Products with disinfecting action may contain antimicrobial agents. When quaternary ammonium salts are used for this purpose, the products are often acidic and may contain strong acids such as hydrochloric acid. Products containing chlorine bleaching agents contain alkalis such as sodium hydroxide, sodium metasilicate, or sodium carbonate. Most toilet bowl cleaners contain a pleasing fragrance.

Because of the incompatible nature of these products, manufacturers often warn consumers not to mix the products.

Related Terms: Bleach, Cleanser, Sequestering Agent, Specialty Cleaning Products, Surface Active Agent

UNBUILT DETERGENT

A detergent without a builder.

Practically all light duty detergents fall in the unbuilt category, as do types of liquid laundry detergents that are unbuilt but also heavy duty.

Related Terms: Heavy Duty Detergent, Laundry Detergent, Light Duty Detergent

WASHING SODA

A common name for a commercial form of hydrated sodium carbonate. It is also called "sal soda" and "soda." Washing soda is often used as a detergent booster.

Related Terms: Sodium Carbonate

WATER HARDNESS

Soluble metal salts, principally those of calcium and magnesium and sometimes iron and manganese, that when present in water in sufficient amount create cleaning problems.

In the case of soap, insoluble soap curds are formed. In general, water hardness reduces the ability of surfactants to perform their cleaning function.

Hardness is expressed in grains per gallon (gpg), grains per liter (gpl), or parts per million (ppm), the last more accurately being expressed as milligrams per liter. One gpg equals 17.1 ppm. Water essentially free of calcium and magnesium is described as soft; if appreciable amounts of either or both are present, it is called hard. The U.S. Geological Survey categories of hardness are:

	Soft	*Moderately hard*	*Hard*	*Very hard*
grains per gallon	0.0–3.5	3.6–7.0	7.1–10.5	10.6+
grains per liter	0.0–.89	.90–1.76	1.77–2.64	2.65+
part per million or miligrams per liter	0.0–60	61–120	121–180	more than 180

Related Terms: Detergent, Soap, Water Softener

WATER SOFTENER

An agent that inactivates or removes water hardness minerals, principally calcium and magnesium and to a lesser degree, iron and manganese.

There are three basic ways to soften water in the home:
— A mechanical water softener - a system tied into the water line that actually removes the hardness minerals.
— Packaged chemical water softeners - classified either as nonprecipitating softeners that sequester hardness minerals, or as precipitating products that remove hardness by forming insoluble compounds.
— Built detergents - in which the softener is incorporated in the washing product.

Mechanical softening operates on what is known as an ion-exchange system, in which hardness minerals are removed from the water and replaced by sodium. The ion-exchange system is regenerated by treatment with a salt. Packaged chemical water softeners of the sequestering type are usually based on complex

Glossary

phosphates; the precipitating kind is based on sodium carbonate and trisodium phosphate.

Related Terms: Phosphates, Precipitating Agent, Sequestering Agent, Water Conditioner, Water Hardness

WATER TEMPERATURE

Degree of hotness or coldness of water.

Water temperature is considered here only in the context of temperature for laundering and dishwashing. Suggested temperature ranges are:

Hot water . . . . *130°F (54.4°C) or above*
Warm water . . . . *90°F (32.2°C) to 110°F (43.3°C)*
Cold water . . . . *80°F (26.7°C) or colder*

WETTING AGENT

A compound that increases the ability and speed with which a liquid displaces air from a solid surface, thus improving the process of wetting that surface.

Wetting agents are all surfactants. They function by lowering surface and interfacial tension. Soap and detergent surfactants serve as wetting agents in washing products, in addition to their other functions. In automatic dishwashing, nonionic surfactants are sometimes introduced into the last rinse for the purpose of maximizing drainage of water from dishes and utensils.

Related Terms: Rinse Agent, Surface Active Agent

Additional References

American Furniture Manufacturers Association, P. O. Box HP-7, High Point, North Carolina 27261, (919) 884-5000

American Home Economics Association, Sales Office, 2010 Massachusetts Avenue, NW, Washington, DC 20036 (Textile Handbook), 1-800-424-8080

American Sheep Producers Council, Inc., 200 Clayton Street, Denver, Colorado 80206, (303) 399-8130

Association of Home Appliance Manufacturers (AHAM), 20 N. Wacker Drive, Chicago, Illinois 60606, (312) 984-5858

Major Appliance Consumer Action Panel (MACAP), 20 N. Wacker Drive, Chicago, Illinois 60606, (312) 984-5858

Man-Made Fiber Producers Association, Inc., 1150 - 17th St. N.W., Washington, DC 20036, (202) 296-6508

National Housewares Manufacturers Association, 1324 Merchandise Mart, Chicago, Illinois 60654, (312) 644-3333

Soap and Detergent Association, 475 Park Avenue, South, New York, New York 10016, (212) 725-1262

Facts About Procter & Gamble

Headquarters: One Procter & Gamble Plaza, Cincinnati, Ohio
(Mail Address: P.O. Box 599, Cincinnati, Ohio 45201)

Founded 1837

Incorporated 1890

U.S. Plant Cities for P&G Laundering, Cleaning and Dishwashing Products

Alexandria, Louisiana
Augusta, Georgia
Baltimore, Maryland
Chicago, Illinois
Cincinnati, Ohio
  Ivorydale
  St. Bernard
Dallas, Texas

Kansas City, Kansas
Lima, Ohio
Long Beach, California
Quincy, Massachusetts
Sacramento, California
St. Louis, Missouri
Staten Island, New York

Research and Development/Engineering Facilities for Laundering, Cleaning and Dishwashing Products

Cincinnati, Ohio:
  Miami Valley Laboratories—applied research
  Ivorydale Technical Center—product development and engineering
  Sharon Woods Technical Center—product development and engineering
  Winton Hill Technical Center—product development and engineering

Olive Branch, Mississippi:
  Home Care Products—applied research, product development and engineering

Brussels, Belgium:
  European Technical Center—product development and engineering

Hamilton, Ontario, Canada:
  product development and engineering

Newcastle, England:
  applied research, product development and engineering

Others:
  Many of the Company's other subsidiaries outside the U.S. also have product development laboratories and engineering facilities.

INDEX

A

Abrasive minerals, 24–25, 193–194
Acetate, 50–51
Acid, 194
Acid-based cleaning products, 123
Acrilan, 52–53
Acrylic, 52–53
Adhesive tape, removal of, 80
Advertising, as source of brand information, 14
Agitation
  choosing proper, 42
  getting information on, from care label, 48
Air drying, to check for stain removal, 39
  dishes, 141
Air freshener/deodorizer, 193, 197
Alcohol, as processing aid, 26
Alcohol, stain removal of, 80
Alkali, 194
Alkalinity, 194
Alkane sulfonate, 196
Alkyl dimethyl benzyl ammonium chloride, 200
Alkyl ethoxylate sulfate, 196
Alkyl glyceryl sulfonate, 196
Alkyl sulfate, 196
All-purpose cleaning products, 128–129, 195, 197
All-purpose detergents, 194–195
Alpha olefin sulfate, 196
Aluminosilicate, 22
Aluminum
  dishwashing of, 152–153, 168–169
  darkened, 150–151, 152–153
  hard surface cleaning of, 116–117
Ammonia, 132–133, 195
Amphoteric, 220
Amylase, 24, 213
Anionic, 22–23, 220

Anionic surfactant, 195–196, 220
Anodized aluminum, cleaning of, 152–153, 168–169
Anso, 54–55
Antimicrobial ingredients, 205
Antiperspirants stain, removal of, 81
Anti-redeposition agents, 24–25
Anti-tarnish lacquer, 155
Antron, 54–55
Aramid, 52–53
Ariloft, 50–51
Arnel, 50–51
Asphalt, cleaning, 112–113
Asphalt tile, 113
Automatic dishwasher
  cleaning interior, 116, 118–121, 122
  cleaning products for, 20, 144–145, 185, 196–197
  cost of operating, 181–182
  hand products use in, 185
  odor in, 168–169
  problems and solutions, 162–169
  questions on use of, 185
  rinse agents, 146–147
  specialty products, 146–147
  washing dishes by, 140–142, 152–161
Avlin, 54–55
Avril, 50–51
Avron, 50–51

B

Baby clothes, washing, 60–61, 178
Bactericide, 206
Baked clay dinnerware, cleaning of, 155
Baked-on food, as hand dishwashing problem, 150–151
Baking soda, 132, 151, 193, 197
Ballpoint ink, stain removal of, 82
Barbeque grill, cleaning, 109

Bathroom
  carpeting/throw rugs, 60–61
  cleaning, 112–113, 120, 184
  fixture cleaning, 112–113, 114, 120, 122–123, 134–135, 221
  guide for general care of, 6–7
  products for cleaning, 128–129, 130–131, 134–135, 197
Bathtub, cleaning, 112–113, 120–123
Beau-Grip, 50–51
Bedroom, guide for general care of, 6–7
Bedspreads, laundering of, 62–63
Belts, buckling while sorting, 36
Beverages, stain removal of, 80
Biodegradability, 23, 198
Biz, 20, 90, 92, 180, 181
Blankets, laundering of, 62–63
Bleach, 20, 38–39, 132–133, 198
  chlorine, 24–25, 39, 60–61, 88–89, 132–133, 180–181, 198, 201, 210, 213
  hints for using, 89
  information on, on care label, 48, 180
  oxygen, 90–91, 151, 180–181
  for stain removal, 38–39
  warning about mixing with cleaners, 88, 133, 182
Bleaching, 198
Blood, stain removal of, 80, 180
Blue "C", 54–55
Blue stains, laundering solution for, 98–99
Bluing, 90–91, 199, 205
Bold 3, 20, 86–87
Boosters, 199
Borax, 193, 200, 208, 213
Bottle brush, 149
Bounce, 20, 90–93
Brands, getting information on, 14–15

227

Brass, cleaning, 116–117
Brighteners. *See* Fluorescent whitening agents
Brown stains, laundering solution for, 98–99
Builders, 22–23, 197, 199–200, 208, 212, 213
Built detergent, 200, 208
Burned-on food, as hand dishwashing problem, 150–151

C
Calcite, 193
Calcium carbonate, 201
Camay, 87
Candle wax, stain removal of, 80
Cantrece, 54–55
Caprolan, 54–55
Carbonates, 22
Carboxymethylcellulose (CMC), 24, 219
Care label
 apparel care labeling guide, 47–49
 alternate cleaning procedure, 47
 bleach statement, 48
 drying instructions, 43, 49
 ironing/pressing statement, 49
 machine cycle statement, 48
 reading and following, 34–35
 special washing/handling statement, 48
 water temperature statement, 47
Carpet cleaners, 128–129
Cascade, 20, 144, 152, 177–178, 184–185
Casseroles, cleaning of, 150–151
Castile, 190
Cast iron
 cleaning of, 152–153
 damage to, 168–169
Catalysts, 180
Cationics, 22–23, 220
Cationic surfactants, 200
Celanese, 50–51
Cellulosic fibers, 50–51
Ceramics, cleaning, 112–114
Ceramic tile, cleaning, 112–113
Chalk, stain removal of, 80
Cheer, 20, 43, 86, 87, 91
Chewing gum, stain removal of, 80
China
 cleaning of, 152–155, 185
 cleaning problems, 168–169

Chipping of dishes, 168–169
Chlorinated isocyanurate, 201
Chlorinated trisodium phosphate, 24, 201
Chlorine bleach, 24–25, 39, 88–89, 132–133, 147, 180–181, 198, 201, 210, 213
 warning on combining with ammonia/acid products, 88, 133
Chocolate, stain removal of, 80
Chrome, cleaning, 182
Chrome plated steel, cleaning, 116–117
Chromspun, 50–51
Cleaning
 consumer questions about, 182–184
 processes involved, 12–13
 tips for, 109–110
Cleaning cloths, laundering of, 64–65
Cleaning products, 20
 all-purpose cleaners, 128–129
 carpet cleaners, 128–129
 carpet fresheners, 128–129
 cleansers, 128–129
 disinfectants, 130–131
 drain cleaners, 130–131
 glass cleaners, 130–131
 ingredients in, 22–29
 insecticides, 130–131
 metal cleaners, 130–131
 oven cleaners, 130–131
 polishes, 134–135
 Procter & Gamble, 20
 questions about, 177–178
 toilet bowl cleaners, 132–133
 traditional cleaners, 132–133
 tub, tile, and sink cleaners, 134–135
 upholstery cleaners, 134–135
 waxes, 134–135
Cleansers, 20, 31, 128–129, 178, 184
Coast, 87
Coffee stains
 as problem, 150–151, 184
 stain removal of, 80
Collar soil, stain removal of, 81
Color, sorting clothes by, 36
Colorants, 24–25
Coloray, 50–51
Color fading, problem of, 102–103
Colorfastness, 36, 181
Color remover, 82
Comet, 20, 121, 128–129, 133, 178, 182–184
Comet Liquid, 20, 178, 182–183

Comforters, laundering of, 62–63
Complex phosphates, 22, 191, 197, 199–200
Concrete, cleaning, 114–115
Consumer Information Services
 at Procter & Gamble, 19–20, 173, 176, 177
 getting product information from, 19–20
 role of, in product development, 173, 176
 as source of brand information, 14
Conventional vinyl flooring, cleaning, 125
Cookware, cleaning, 150–151
Copper
 dishwashing of, 154–155
 hard surface cleaning of, 116–117
Cork, cleaning, 114–115
Corrosion inhibitor, 24–25, 197, 201–202
Cosmetics, stain removal of, 81
Cotton, 56–57
Coupons, as source of brand information, 14
Crayon, stain removal of, 81
Creslan, 52–53
Cuff soil, stain removal of, 81
Curtains, laundering of, 64–65

D
Dacron, 54–55
Daily chores
 for clothing care and laundering, 8
 for general home care, 6–7
Dash, 20, 86–87
Dawn, 20, 43, 139, 144–145, 178, 185
Delicate fabrics, laundering of, 66–67
Deodorants, stain removal of, 81
Detergency, 202
Detergent, 202–203, 208
 all-purpose, 195
 amount to use, 40–41, 179
 built, 200, 208
 development of, 191–192
 heavy duty, 86–87, 207
 light duty, 86–87, 144–145, 209
 liquid, 210–211
 synthetic, 191, 220–221
 unbuilt, 209, 221
Detergent boosters, 90–91

Diapers
    laundering of, 60–61
    soaking, 213
Dichloroisocyanurate, 24
Dishcloth, 149
Dish drainer, 149
Dishpan, 149
Dish towels, 149
Dishwashing
    by automatic dishwasher, 140–142
        problems, 162–169
    consumer questions regarding, 184–185
    dishwashable items, 152–161
    by hand, 139–140
        problems, 150–151
        supplies, 149
    organizing for, 138–139
    Procter & Gamble products, 20
    products and aids, 20, 144–147
        ingredients in, 22–29
    reasons for, 137–138
Disinfectants, 130–131, 203
Dispersing, 13
Down-filled items, laundering of, 66–67
Downy, 20, 90–91
Drainboard, 149
Drain cleaners, 130–131
Draperies, laundering of, 64–65
Dreft, 20, 43, 86, 191
Drying information
    checking care label for, 43, 49
    special instructions for, 60–77
Durvil, 50–51
Dye transfer, stain removal of, 82

E
Earthenware, cleaning of, 154–155
EDTA, 207
Elasticized apparel, laundering of, 66–67
Electric blankets, laundering of, 68–69
Emulsifying, 12
Encron, 54–55
Enkalure, 54–55
Enkasheer, 54–55
Enkrome, 50–51
Enzymes, 24–25, 37, 180, 203–204, 213
Era Plus, 20, 86, 87, 91, 180

Estron, 50–51
Etching, 155, 168, 204
Eutrophication, 204–205

F
Fabric, sorting clothes by, 36
Fabric abrasion, laundering solution for, 100–101
Fabric discoloration, laundering solution for, 98–99
Fabric freshener/deodorizer, 193
Fabric finishes and sizing, 92–93
Fabric softener, 20, 90–93, 205
    dryer-added, 90–93, 205
    ingredients in, 26–27, 205
    consumer questions about, 181
    rinse-added, 90–91, 205
    stain removal of, 82, 91
    wash-added, 90–91, 92, 205
Family room, guide for general care of, 6–7
Feces, stain removal of, 85
Federal Trade Commission, care labels, 34, 47
Feldspar, 24, 193, 201
Felt tip marker, stain removal of, 82
Fiber facts, 50–59
Fiberglass, 52–53
    cleaning of, 120
Filming, 150–151, 162–165, 168–169, 185
    removal of, 155
Floors, cleaning tips, 109
Fluorescent whitening agents, 26–27, 205–206
Fortrel, 54–55
Fragrance, in cleaning products, 26–27, 197
Freezers
    baking soda as deodorizer for, 197
    cleaning exterior of, 122–123
    cleaning interior of, 118–119
Fruit juice, stain removal of, 82
Fungi removal, 198
FWA's. *See* Fluorescent whitening agents

G
Gain, 20, 86
Garment construction, sorting clothes by, 36

Germicide, 206
Glass
    breaking and chipping of, 166–167
    dishwashing of, 154–155
    film and spots on, 150–151, 168–169, 185, 205
        solution for, 155
    hard surface cleaning of, 114–115, 183
    products for, 130–131
Glass ceramics, cleaning of, 150–151, 154–155
Glass fiber, 52–53
Glospan, 56–57
Granules, 206
Grass, stain removal of, 82
Gray, black or metal marks
    as automatic dishwasher problem, 166–167
    as hand dishwashing problem, 150–151
Grayness, laundering solution for, 96–97
Grease stains
    laundering problem, 98–101
    stain removal of, 82
Grouting, cleaning of, 112
Gunther, Fritz, 191
Gym shoes, laundering of, 74–75

H
Hand dishwashing, 139–140
    problems and solutions, 150–151
    products for, 20, 144–145
    supplies for, 149
Hand laundry, 43–44
Hard surface cleaning, 107–110
Hard water. *See* Water hardness
Heavy duty detergents, 86–87, 207
Heavy-soiled clothes, laundering of, 68–69
Herculon, 54–55
Holes, laundering problem, 102–103
Home care, guide for general, 6–7
Hooks, closing in sorting, 36
Hosiery, laundering of, 70–71
Household ammonia, 195
Household bleach, 210
Household cleaner, 207
Hydrated sodium carbonate, 221
Hydrochloric acid, 221

Hydrogen peroxide, 211
Hydrolysis, 216
Hydrophilic, 23, 207
Hydrophobic, 23, 207
Hypochlorite, 201

I
Incipient etching, 204
Ink, stain removal of, 82
Insecticides, 130–131
Iodine, stain removal of, 83
Ion exchange, 22
Ion-exchange system, 222
Iridescence/coating, 168–169
Ironing information, on care label, 49
Ivory Liquid, 20, 43, 139, 144–145, 178, 185
Ivory Snow, 20, 86
Ivory Soap Bar, 86, 91, 171, 180

J
Jogging shoes, laundering of, 74–75
Joy, 20, 139, 144–145, 178, 185

K
Kevlar, 52–53
Kitchen
  appliance cleaning, 116–123
  guide for general care of, 6–7
Kodel, 54–55

L
Laundering, 33–34
  consumer questions regarding, 177–182
  correct amount of detergent, 179
  drying clothes properly, 43
  following package directions, 40–41
  guide for, 8–9
  by hand, 43–44
  pretreating soils and stains, 37–39
  problem solving, 96–105
  products, 20, 86–87
    aids, 88–95, 208
    bluings, 90–91, 199, 205
    chlorine bleach, 24–25, 39, 88–89, 132–133, 147, 180–181, 198, 201, 210, 213
    detergent boosters, 90–91
    detergents, 86–87, 208
    fabric finishes and sizing, 92–93
    fabric softeners, 90–93
    heavy duty detergents, 86–87, 207
    ingredients in, 22–29
    light duty detergents, 86–87, 144–145, 209
    light duty soaps, 86–87, 209
    oxygen bleach, 26–27, 90–91, 180–181, 198, 211
    presoak agents, 92–93
    Procter & Gamble products, 20
    soap bars, 86–87, 208–209
    soil and stain removers, 79, 92–93
    starches, 92–93
    water softeners, 94–95
  proper washing action, 42
  proper water temperature, 41–42, 233
  read and follow care labels, 34–35, 47–49
  rinsing thoroughly, 42
  rules for, 33–43
  size of wash loads, 37
  sorting, 35–37
  special instructions, 60–77
Leblanc, Nicolas, 190
Light duty detergents, 209
  for laundry, 86–87
  for dishwashing, 144–145
Light duty soaps, 86–87, 209
Lime soap, 209–210
Limestone, 24
Linear alkylate sulfonate, 196
Linen, 56–57
Lingerie, laundering of, 70–71
Linoleum, cleaning, 114–115
Lint-producing fabrics, separating, 36
Lint removal, 100–103
Liquid Bold 3, 20, 86, 91, 180
Liquid Cascade, 20, 144
Liquid Cheer, 20, 86, 91, 180
Liquid detergent, 210–211
Liquid Tide, 20, 86–87, 180, 187
Living room, guide for general care of, 6–7
Loftura, 50–51
Lycra, 56–57

M
Man-made fibers, 50–57
  Cellulosic, 50
  Non-Cellulosic, 51–57
Manufacturer
  getting product information from, 19–20
  as source of brand information, 14
Marble, cleaning, 124–125
Marks on dishes, 150–151, 166–167
Marquesa Lana, 54–55
Mattress covers/pads, laundering of, 70–71
Mechanical water softeners, 95
Melamin, cleaning, 157
Mending, while sorting, 37
Metals, cleaning
  common, 116–117
  special, 116–117
Metal cleaners, 130–131
Methylcellulose, 24
Microwave ovens, cleaning, 118, 120
Mildew, stain removal of, 83, 198
Minimum care vinyl, cleaning, 125
Modacrylic fiber, 52–53
Mr. Clean, 20, 128, 178, 182–184
Mr. Clean Cleanser, 20, 121, 128–129, 182–183
Mucus, stain removal of, 85
Mud, stain removal of, 83
Multisheer, 54–55
Mustard, stain removal of, 83

N
Nail polish, stain removal of, 83
Natural fibers, 56–59
Nomex, 52–53
Non-cellulosic fiber, 52–57
Nonionics, 22–23, 220
Nonionic surfactant, 211
Nonstick cookware, cleaning, 150–151, 156–157
No-wax flooring, 124
  cleaning, 125, 183
Numa, 56–57
Nylon, 54–55

O
Occasional chores
  for clothing care and laundering, 8–9
  for general home care, 6–7

Oil-based cosmetic stains, removal of, 81
Oil-based paint stains, removal of, 83
Oil stains
  laundering solution for, 98–101
  removal of, 82
Olefin, 54–55
Opacifiers, 26–27
Orion, 52–53
Oven cleaning, 118, 120, 122
  cleaners for, 21, 130–131
  racks, 109, 122
Oxidizing agent, 197
Oxydol, 20, 40, 86, 181
Oxygen bleach, 26–27, 90–91, 180–181, 198, 211

P

Package
  as source of brand information, 15
  as source of use instruction, 40–41
  diagram of, 16–17
Packaged water softener, 95
Painted steel, cleaning, 116–117
Painted surfaces, cleaning, 118–119, 183
Paint, stain removal of, 83
Patlon, 54–55
People-power, making good use of, 4
Perborate, 211
Permanent press, laundering of, 72–73, 104–105
Perspiration, stain removal of, 84, 195
Pewter, cleaning, 156–157
Phenolic compounds, 203
Phosphate bans, 186–187
Pilling, 104–105
Pillows, laundering of, 72–73
Pine oil, 212
Pine oil products, 203, 212
Pitting, 153, 166–167
Plan, making, 3–4
Plastic(s)
  dishwashing of, 156–157
  distortion of, 168–169
  hard surface cleaning, 118–121
  laundering of, 74–75
Plastic scrubbers, 149
Plastic spatula, 149
Pockets, turning inside out, in sorting, 36
Polishes, 134–135

Polyacrylates, 24
Polyester, 54–55
Polyethoxylated imines, 24
Polyethylene glycol, 24
Polyvinyl acetate, 219
Poor soil removal, laundering solution for, 98–99
Porcelain, cleaning, 122–123, 184
Porcelain enamel, cleaning, 158–159
Potash, 190
Potassium monopersulfate, 211
Potassium pyrophosphate, 207
Pottery, cleaning, 154–155
Precipitating, 22–23
Presoaking, 213
Presoak products, 92–93, 213–214
Pressing information. See Ironing information
Pretreating soils and stains, 37–39, 214
  pretreat, 38
  prewash, 37
  products for, 79, 92–93
  soak, 37
  spotting, 218
  tips for, 38–39
Prewash, 37, 214
Prices, effect of, on product choice, 15
Priorities, determining, 3–4
Processing aids, 26–27, 197
Procter & Gamble (P&G)
  Consumer Services, 19–20, 173
  consumer questions, 177–187
  facts about, 225
  product development, 171–176
  toll-free 800-lines, 20
Products
  categories of, 31
  choice of, 11–13
  consumer questions regarding, 177–187
  development of, 171–176
  getting information on, 14–15, 19–20
  ingredients, 22–29
  taking questions to manufacturer, 19–20
  testing of, 174–176
  tips on storage, 15, 18
Protease, 24, 213
Protein-based stains, 37, 180
Pumice, 193

Q

Quartz, 193
Quaternary ammonium compounds, 200, 203, 220
Quaternary ammonium salts, 26, 28, 221

R

Ramie, 56–57
Ranges, cleaning, 122, 128–129
Rayon, 50–51
Refrigerator
  cleaning exterior of, 122–123
  cleaning interior of, 118–119
  use of baking soda as deodorizer for, 197
Residue, laundering solution for, 100–101
Rinse agents, for automatic dishwashers, 146–147, 215
Rinsing, 42–43
Room freshener/deodorizer, 193
Rubber
  cleaning, 124–125
  fiber, 54–55
Rubber cement, stain removal of, 80
Rubberized fabrics, laundering of, 74–75
Rubber spatula, 149
Rubber tile, 125
Rust remover, 215
Rust
  laundering solution for, 98–99
  stain removal of, 84

S

Safeguard, 87
Sal soda, 221
Samples, as source of product information, 14, 175
Sand, as an abrasive, 193
Sanitizer, 215
Saponification, 216
Sashes, tying when sorting, 36
Scorch marks, stain removal of, 84
Scratching, and hard surface cleaning, 110
Seasonal chores
  for clothing care and laundering, 8
  for general home care, 6–7
SEF fibers, 52–53

Septic tanks, safety of P & G products for, 186
Sequestering, 13, 22–23, 212
Sequestering agent, 216
Shareen, 54–55
Shoes, laundering of, 74–75
Shrinking, 104–105
Silica, 24, 201
Silicates, 22
Silk, 58–59
Silverplate, cleaning, 158–159, 166–167
Silverstone, cleaning of, 156–157
Silverware drainer, 149
Sink mat, 149
Sinks, cleaning, 112–113, 116–117, 120–123
Sink stopper, 149
Size of item, sorting clothes by, 36
Snags, 102–103
Soaking, 37. *See also* Presoaking
    need for, in cleaning hard surfaces, 109
Soap(s)s, 20, 216–217
    bars, 86–87, 208–209
    early American, 190–191
    French influence, 190
    history of, 189
    light duty, 86–87, 209
    lime, 209–210
Soap curd, 217
Soap pads, 193, 195
Soda ash, 217
Sodium aluminosilicate, 199
Sodium bicarbonate, 213
Sodium carbonate, 199, 200, 208, 211, 213, 217, 221
Sodium citrate, 200, 213, 217
Sodium hexametaphosphate (SHMP), 212
Sodium hydroxide, 28, 221
Sodium hypochlorite, 201, 210
Sodium metaphosphate, 221
Sodium metasilicate, 221
Sodium orthophosphate, 212
Sodium perborate, 211, 213
Sodium perborate tetrahydrate, 26
Sodium percarbonate, 211
Sodium silicate, 24, 197, 200, 208, 213, 217
Sodium sulfate, 26, 218
Sodium tripolyphosphate, 191–192, 200, 212, 213
Soft drink, stain removal of, 80

Soil, sorting clothes by kind and amount, 36
Solo, 20, 86–87, 91, 180
Solvent sensitive ink, stain removal of, 82
Sorting of clothes, 35–37
    by color, 36
    by fabric, 36
    by garment construction, 36
    hints in proper, 36–37
    by size of item, 36
    by soil in clothes, 36
Spandex, 56–57
Special washing/handling, information on, on care label, 48
Special ingredients, 28–29
Spic and Span, 20, 128–129, 178, 182–183
Spic and Span Pine Liquid, 20, 128–129, 130, 178, 182–183
Spotting
    in dishwashing, 146–147, 155, 162–165
    in laundry pretreatment, 218. *See also* Stain removal
Stain(s), 218
Stainless steel
    cleaning, 116–117, 158–159
    pitting of, 153, 166–167
Stain removal
    guide for specific stains, 80–85
    procedures for, 79
    products for, 31, 79, 92–93
    tips on, 38–39
Starch, 92–93, 218–219
Starch-based stains, 37
Static control agents, 26–27
Steel wool pads, 149
Sterling silver, cleaning, 160–161, 164–165
Stone, cleaning, 124–125
Stoneware, cleaning of, 155, 160–161
Stool, stain removal of, 85
Storage, tips on, 15, 18
Stoves
    cleaning oven, 109, 118–123, 130–131
    cleaning range top, 122, 128–129
Suds, 219
Suds control agents, 28–29
Suds stabilizers, 28–29
Suds suppressors, 28–29, 197
Surface active agent, 219–220

Surfactants, 22–23, 195–200, 208, 211, 219–221, 223
Synthetic detergents, 220–221

T

Table linens, laundering of, 76–77
Tar, stain removal of, 84
Tears, 102–103
Tea stains
    as hand dishwashing problem, 150–151
    stain removal of, 80
Teflon, cleaning of, 156–157
Terrazzo, cleaning, 124–125
Tetrapotassium pyrophosphate, 212
Tetrasodium pyrophosphate, 212
Thermosetting plastics, cleaning, 156–157
Tide, 20, 86–87, 180, 187, 192
    diagram of package, 16–17
Timetable, making out a, 4
Tobacco, stain removal of, 85
Toilet bowl cleaning, 112–114
    bowl fresheners, 133
    cleaners, 132–133, 197, 221
Toll-free P&G phone numbers, 20
Top Job, 20, 128, 178, 182–183
Traditional cleaners, 132–133
Tree sap, stain removal of, 84
Triacetate, 50–51
Trichloroisocyanuric acid, 24
Trisodium phosphate, 212
Trivira, 54–55
Tub, tile and sink cleaners, 134–135
Typewriter correction fluid, stain removal of, 85

U

Unbuilt detergent, 209
U.S. Environmental Protection Agency, 203
Upholstery cleaners, 134–135
Urine, stain removal of, 85

V

Vegetable starch, 218–219
Vinegar
    for cleaning, 132–133
    for laundry problems, 98–101
    for dishwasher problems, 147, 155

Vinyl, cleaning, 124–125
Vomit, stain removal of, 85

W

Wallpaper, cleaning, 126–127
Washing machine. *See also* Laundering
    cost of operating, 181–182
    choosing proper washing action, 42, 48
Washing soda, 221
Wash loads, planning to conserve water, 37
Water-based cosmetic, stain removal of, 81
Water-based paint, stain removal of, 83
Water hardness, 9, 40–41, 222
    and amount of detergent, 163, 179
Water sensitive ink, stain removal of, 82

Water softeners, 94–95, 222–223
Water temperature, 223
    checking care label for proper, 47
    cold, 42, 47, 178–179, 223
    hot, 41, 47, 223
    for rinsing, 42, 179
    warm, 41–42, 47, 223
Waxes, 134–135
Waxing
    and floor care, 113–114, 124–125
    of furniture, 126–127
Weekly chores
    for clothing care and laundering, 8
    for general home care, 6–7
Wetting, 12, 220
Wetting agent, 223
Windows, cleaning, 183
Wood
    cleaning, 126–127, 183
    dishwashing, 160–161, 168–169
Wool, 58–59
    laundering of, 62–63

Work clothes, laundering of, 68–69
Wrinkling, 104–105, 179

X

Xylan, cleaning of, 156–157

Y

Yellowing, laundering solution for, 96–97
Yellow stains, laundering solution for, 98–99

Z

Zantrel, 50–51
Zefkrome, 52–53
Zefran, 52–53, 54–55
Zest, 87
Zippers, closing in sorting, 36

Personal Notes

Personal Notes

Personal Notes

Personal Notes

Personal Notes

Personal Notes

Personal Notes

Personal Notes

Personal Notes

Personal Notes